St. Amel
Liturgy C

Motivating Your Parish to Change

Concrete Leadership Strategies
for Pastors, Administrators,
and Lay Leaders

Rev. David Heney

Resource Publications, Inc.
San Jose, California

Reprint Department
Resource Publications, Inc.
160 E. Virginia Street #290
San Jose, CA 95112-5876
(408) 286-8505 (voice)
(408) 287-8748 (fax)

Library of Congress Cataloging-in-Publication Data
Heney, David, 1952–
   Motivating your parish to change : concrete leadership strategies for pastors, administrators, and lay leaders / David Heney.
      p.   cm.
   ISBN 0-89390-433-3
   1. Christian leadership. 2. Pastoral theology. 3. Change-Religious aspects—Christianity. I. Title.
BV652.1.H445   1998
253—dc21   98-5005
                                              CIP

Printed in the United States of America.
98 99 00 01 02 | 5 4 3 2 1

Editorial director: Nick Wagner
Project manager: Mike Sagara
Copyeditor: Robin Witkin

Author photograph © copyright by Maria Karras Photography, Pasadena, Calif.

Contents

3. Getting Started on the Journey

4. Staying In Charge of the Journey

Preface

Ministry is a joy. Well, maybe ministry is difficult. Which describes your experience? More likely, you might oscillate between these descriptions depending on the circumstances of your day. Of course, I hope your ministry is a joyful and satisfying experience. For too many, though, ministry is becoming a serious challenge. It is becoming more difficult to live with any kind of joy. This book would like to change that.

If you are a parish leader in these post–Vatican II times, you have a lot of challenges. Whether you're the pastor, associate, school principal, teacher, or in charge of some parish ministry team, you deal in important ways with people. You are in charge, and that carries a great responsibility. How will you lead? How will you get your ideas across? How will you treat people? Today, so many people involved in church activities are volunteers. They just cannot be ordered around, no matter how good the orders are. Keeping their loyalty and energy high involves different skills than those used with paid staff. Of course, parishioners are also, in a sense, volunteers. They don't have to be involved at all. People often ignore parish boundaries and go where they like, and that is a new challenge for leaders today.

Motivating and leading people is no easy task, even for "born leaders" who seem so natural at it. Not everyone succeeds. Unfortunately, there are too many stories of parish leaders "burning out" and leaving ministry after just a short time of service. Leading the people of your parish that you love so much can be frustrating, confusing, and stressful. Let's face it, being in charge of people can be dangerous to your health! If you are in any kind of leadership position in the parish at all, this book is written for you.

Certainly, the first apostles found leading people challenging, but today that task seems even more complex. While we may want to go "into the whole world and baptize all nations," sometimes we're not exactly sure how to accomplish it. After all, the world changes so quickly. What worked well in one era may produce little benefit in the next. And for that matter, what does it really mean to go "into the world" anyway? What kind of world is it today? How can we bring people to Christ in the best possible way, and in a way that is both genuine and real? Even more important, how can we do it in the way God wants? We parish leaders ask those questions precisely because we love the Lord and believe in him. We ask because we want to continue his mission, and we want to do it well.

We live in a cynical age. Our society does not look kindly on leaders, authorities, or institutions. Numerous studies and opinion polls have shown that people are disappointed in government leaders, are angry at greedy business managers, and are shocked by the personal scandals of those in high places. There is an almost automatic resistance to any person who dares tell us what to do. The goodness of the message becomes lost in our general mistrust of institutional authority. Yet we can really accomplish nothing as a people of God without effective leaders who know what they are doing and who can lead well. Ironically, we can use this very mistrust as a spur to energize our own desire to succeed. Now more than ever, we need effective leadership to turn mistrust into confidence and hope for the future. Now is an important time for leaders to lead well. Let us rediscover good leadership as God intended it to be.

These reflections will look at the ministry of parish leaders in difficult and changing times and offer some guidelines for working with people more effectively. These ideas will be more than just clever management techniques or organizational tricks of the business world. After all, our life is more than just a job. Our ministry is more than just good business practice. We need a model of service that is not only authentic to the Gospel but also a joy to live. We need a way to work joyfully, even in these difficult times, that is still faithful to our best Christian traditions. Of course, every age in church history has had its problems, but this present time is our time and involves us, so we need to address the issues for ministers today.

This is not a book on the spirituality or faith-development of leaders. Of course, our relationship with God and our spiritual life are of paramount importance. Of course, our faith must be the core of all we do. However, there are many books on spirituality for ministers already. That aspect of parish leadership is very well covered by literally thousands of authors, workshops, and seminars. Nevertheless, we need to know both the vertical dimension of faith *and* the horizontal dimension of organizational dynamics. This book adds to the field by addressing the human side of leadership. It addresses those human dynamics that occur when one person attempts to influence the actions of another. "Grace builds on nature." This book is about human nature and what happens when we attempt to lead others in accord with the grace of God.

There are many ways of organizing this material, but it is not meant to be just another book on management technique. Nevertheless, this book will draw on some of those management ideas simply because they are effective. Certainly, terms like *quality, customer service,* and *job satisfaction* are hot topics in business today, especially in this era of global competition. The power of today's fiercely competitive business climate has forced many American companies to isolate more precisely just what the factors are for commercial success. American consumers have many product options before them, and only certain effective companies will succeed in capturing the elusive American consumer. Well, we are competing as well in a religiously pluralistic society. People today tend to "shop around" for the best church experiences. Our people have many religious options before them, so we need to be organized just as well as a business to succeed. We want our people to experience the faith as clearly as possible so that the voice of God comes through clearly to them. While we believe it is the Lord who calls people to himself, we also believe he calls us to do our part as well.

We can no longer take effective ministry, or people, for granted. As a church, we can isolate those human factors from our own tradition and those that God has used to help the church grow in ages past. We believe we can discover unique leadership dynamics from our own salvation history that can predict success for our own time. After all, our faith has had a lot of success already. We don't want to lose the valuable examples of heroic leadership from our past. We can listen and learn from Abraham and Moses, from Peter and Paul, and from the Lord himself. The sure and certain minister, joyfully working under the guidance of the Holy Spirit, is our goal. There can be no doubt or confusion concerning our role in this religiously competitive world. The ideas in this book can help any minister answer the provocative and personal question, "What should I be doing around here?"

There is no stronger message of hope in all the Gospels than these wonderful lines from Matthew: "I am with you always, to the end of the age" (28:20). They are just the right words to calm fears about taking on the world. They give us courage but remind us of real work as well. While Jesus is always present to encourage us with his grace and support, there is no doubt the salvation of the world remains a cooperative mission between God and us. Salvation is not automatic, nor, for that matter, is a smoothly working church. There is a real part for us to do. Neither God nor the church work alone, for he needs us as we need him. He simply wants us to do our share.

Because our church has many leadership titles such as bishop, pastor, principal, teacher, and minister, I will use the more generic titles of leader, followers, and workers to simplify discussion. The main subject, however, remains leadership and its crucial place at the center of church life. This book is about the leading of souls. It is addressed to anyone who is in charge, and it invites him or her to take his or her position seriously, for the consequences are serious if that doesn't happen.

Introduction

Good parish leaders have common traits. Struggling ones differ. Good leaders stand together with a certain recognizable sameness of character that ensures success. After all, good work and successful projects have similar characteristics and spring from similar virtues. Only certain qualities enable success. For example, if you remember the best and most effective parish leaders from your own history, you might discern these similar common characteristics about them. Good parish leaders have a certain "energy," even the quiet ones, and can communicate that energy to those around them. They seem focused and clear about what they are doing and can attract others to the path they walk. They possess a certain confidence and courage that carry them and the people they lead through tough moments. They feel as if they are doing something very important and they are excited about finishing it. They want you to join them in the adventure.

Struggling parish leaders are different, each in his or her own way. Failure can take many forms, so the leaders behind failed ministries may seem different from one another. There is a much wider variety of negative personality types, and therefore struggling parish leaders will bring more diverse problems to their ministries. These leaders may be more unfocused, perhaps rapidly shifting from one interest to another. They may be consumed by personal issues that drive them inward in an ever-spiraling, selfish vortex that shuts others out. They may have more malignant personalities that poison relationships and spread dissension in the parish, all for some kind of ill-conceived personal gain. Finally, they may simply be ignorant of anything better, never having noticed there are other, more satisfying ways of doing things. For these and many other reasons, they flounder in their work and sometimes bring the rest of the parish down with them. While there is a sameness to successful personalities, there is a bewildering array of unsuccessful

types. The struggling ones go their own way, and all the paths proceed unhappily.

Of course, we need more happy and successful parish leaders.
We need people who are energetic, focused, and clear about their
mission. We need more parish leaders who love their work, are
effective at making things happen, and generate enthusiastic followers. Most important, we need leaders who are joyful. After all, people like these qualities. We are attracted to people like this and we
want to follow them. Even better, we would like to live the same way
ourselves. How similar to Jesus these good parish leaders seem.

Fortunately, these traits are clearly recognizable and, best of all,
fairly easily learned. The good news is that we can study and learn
them and quickly see good results. Jesus spent his ministry teaching
the apostles these very ideas. We can learn from the Lord how to do
this. The power of the Holy Spirit continues to fire disciples who
have prepared themselves as did those who gathered in the "upper
room" at that first Pentecost. In fact, we can look to the whole of salvation history for numerous examples of motivating ministers.
There is no need to reinvent the wheel. This path has been
walked before.

There are important reasons for motivating our ministries. Successful ministry, good leadership, and effective motivation must be
proactive projects by church leaders, or else we will move backward.
Negative personalities tend to be powerful. Precisely because they
are often driven by selfish or narcissistic needs, negative personalities can be quite insistent and strong. They can confuse any organization quickly. They can exploit, knowingly or not, the fact that no
group can tolerate an absence of direction or leadership. Every
group, organization, family, or parish instinctively looks for direction from someone. Groups abhor a leadership vacuum and will
find someone to fill it. *Unless the virtues of successful ministry are actively
sponsored, encouraged, promoted, taught, and learned by church leaders,
more negative personalities will rise to the top, become influential, and poison the whole system.* Certain negative personalities seek that kind of
control and often get it precisely because of the absence of good
leadership in the parish. *Good leadership principles must be driven from
the top.* It rarely happens from the bottom up. Good leaders must
lead or more negative personalities will.

Parish activities tend to fall into two main categories. There is
the work that comes our way, like weddings, funerals, sick calls, and
counseling, and the work we make ourselves, like fund-raising programs, evangelization projects, and retreats. The first category is

reactive. We respond to someone asking for something. The second category is proactive. We anticipate a need before anyone asks. It is our initiative to work and it does not necessarily have to happen. A parish leader who waits for something to happen is the reactive type. That is not leadership. This book is about taking initiative and proactively working.to make things happen. Positive, proactive, energized leadership anticipates the future and ensures the parish will be ready to meet it. That is a much bigger task than passively waiting for things to take care of themselves. Even though proactive leadership is challenging, we believe it is the mission from our Lord. We will need his help throughout to make it happen.

Motivating people is difficult. Anyone attempting to organize a team project or run a team effort will encounter stress, resistance, and strain. If a leader hopes to survive the process, he or she better know what to do. Without good training, a well-meaning, good-hearted, and sincerely motivated person can quickly become cynical, burned out, and bitter. Groups of people take on certain psychological dynamics that can be powerful and difficult to manage. Unless a solid core of sound leadership and mental health principles is (1) rooted in our Christian faith and (2) lived at the center of the leader's personality, he or she will flounder under the stress of unmanaged, chaotic group dynamics. It would be tragic if the very act of ministry became the cause of failure. Why should a person with a natural desire to do well and serve the Lord be left to flounder for lack of training? Why should willing followers suffer under some selfish autocrat? Neither case has to happen. Even the most challenging situations can be turned around with the application of a few sound ideas.

I hope these reflections will propose a way of doing ministry that will provide a good environment, clear rules, and effective guidelines to allow our natural talent for success to happen easily. While leadership is not automatic, nor magically bestowed by title alone, the principles certainly can be learned. These ideas will ensure that the natural goodness God placed in us will shine in our work. This simple program will work to limit the effectiveness of bad leaders while guiding and encouraging everyone to more effective ministry. Most important, I hope to restore confidence in our ability to accomplish the mission we have from the Lord and in the institutions and leaders he set up to do it.

We can look directly within our own history for the answers. After all, God has already accomplished much with us recalcitrant, stubborn, and rebellious human-types. We can look to actual salvation history examples for the lessons we need in ministry today. What better place to seek wisdom than those moments when God was calling the shots. Specifically, we will examine the Exodus event from the Old Testament and some examples from the life of Jesus and the apostles. Each example deals with motivating people to accomplish a monumental task that, at first glance, seemed impossible. Nothing is impossible with God.

Chapter One

Moses and
the Exodus

Whether you're a parish leader already or just starting out in a new assignment, you are making some kind of change. If you have been a leader for some time, these ideas may inspire you to a new way of doing the same ministry. If you are just beginning, your people will experience a change from their old boss to you, their new boss. Either way there is a transition, a movement from one way or style to another. In his short but very compelling book, *Transitions* (Addison-Wesley Publishing Co., 1991), William Bridges identifies four ideas that leaders use to help people move from one place to another easily and clearly: purpose, picture, planning, and participation. I will borrow them here as we look at change in ministry, especially as seen in the biblical story of Moses and the Exodus. These four words are important to keep in mind because change, or movement, or transition, can either be the most rewarding or the most damaging of human experiences. Rarely has change been written about with such drama and force as in the story of Moses.

What Does a Leader Do?

Moses led thousands of people from a place of slavery, suffering, and pain to a Promised Land in Canaan, a place "flowing with milk and honey." That just doesn't happen very often in history! Moses revealed two basic ideas about leaders in that dramatic exodus event. First, leaders move. They take people someplace new. Leaders *lead* along a certain path and people follow. That new place may be as simple as adopting a new parish liturgy policy or a new religious education program or as complex as building a new church. In every case, leaders move people forward to new ground. Second, leaders create followers. They attract people to themselves who *want* to go to that new place. Leaders actually create or mobilize a *desire* in people to *follow* their lead. No person is truly a leader unless he or she can attract people.

These two ideas differentiate leaders from other influential people like teachers, heroes, and managers. For example, a hero, like Charles Lindbergh, is someone we might admire but do not necessarily follow. After all, heroic deeds like flying the Atlantic solo are not for everyone. On the other hand, a great teacher is someone we might follow but not necessarily admire. Soldiers usually do not like their drill instructors, but they will grudgingly acknowledge the DIs are good teachers and will obey their direction. Finally, managers are people we may or may not admire, but they are not going any place for us to follow anyway. Managers organize, process, or maintain the present system. They do not lead us to anything new. While some use the words *leadership* and *management* interchangeably, they really describe different behaviors.

In this book we will be talking about a special class of leaders, those who take people to a *better* place. We believe leadership is a service, a gift or talent from God that leaders can use for the building of the kingdom of God. This kind of leader acts for the good of the followers and points to a direction that is noble and uplifting. Leaders lead followers to a new and better place.

Leaving one place to travel to another is a powerful metaphor for change, and sometimes it is desperately needed. The Israelites clearly did not like their situation in Egypt. Moses didn't need to remind the people of their pain and suffering under slavery. They wanted out, and they wanted out fast. The *purpose* of the exodus was clear, and at first, it was simply to get out of town! But Moses added several ideas that made the trip more compelling. He revealed the journey as God's will. They were fulfilling some larger plan for the whole world. Most especially, using vivid imagery that captured the imagination of the nation, he painted a *picture* of a bright future back in their old homeland. They would regain their national identity as God's chosen people. Among other things, Moses called Canaan a "land flowing with milk and honey." For people accustomed to making bricks with no straw, that picture fired their souls.

Moses led the Israelites to regain their sense of being a people with a common faith, and it was made concrete in the mission to live in the Promised Land. Most important, he had a *plan* to get there that was simplicity itself. The people were simply to get in line and walk behind him through the desert. Finally, to forge this people into a nation that could inspire other nations, there was a *part* or role for each person to perform. Every Israelite was to faithfully follow the Ten Commandments, which were a clear delineation of the minimum expectations of God. In living the Commandments, they would reveal the true relationship we have with each other and with God to the whole world. They would be his "light to the gentiles." They would be happy. Of course, we are familiar with the story and its significance for our faith, but let us look at the simple psychological significance of leadership and motivation found in it.

What Moses accomplished was incredible. Just consider the events. Moses returned from relative obscurity in the desert of Midian to challenge the mighty Pharaoh of Egypt, the most powerful ruler on earth. Moses organized a dispirited, broken people and was acknowledged as their leader. He was accepted as a prophet of the Lord. He successfully negotiated the people's release from slavery. Moses persuaded ordinary people to follow him into an immense and dangerous desert and to move directly toward a well-known, impassable water barrier. He kept the people's hopes alive even while being pursued by Pharaoh's army, and of course, he accomplished that little task of parting the waters of the Red Sea. Moses was our kind of leader because he took the people to a new and better place. In short, Moses fulfilled the majestic mission given to him by the Lord. These were no small tasks Moses accomplished. Can we learn anything from his success?

Leading with Purpose, Picture, Plan, and Participation

We can identify in this story four words that describe four separate events in motivating any person to undertake a great task. These are the words leaders must keep in mind as they organize change from one way of ministry to another. The first step is to define the *purpose*. People usually don't like change and will resist either openly or secretly any sudden movement or shift in normal operating procedures. Both Pharaoh and the Israelites resisted change at first (Ex 6:5–12). There has to be a good reason for the change to occur or the task to be done, and the leader must explain it well. Our intellect is important and people need to understand *why* a change is good. People will feel emotionally better about something that makes good sense. Of course, both the head and the heart, in a mature balance, must guide our life, but we also need a logical rationale for our efforts. After all, the task must make good common sense.

More important, it has to be a worthy task, and the more difficult the better. We get no thrill from, say, successfully breathing for
a few minutes. As necessary as breathing is, it is not particularly
hard. It is no great accomplishment. Anyone could do it. But we can
feel very proud, say, of reconciling a broken family, or solving a parishioner's complaint, or facing serious illness. Those are harder
tasks. When the task is noble, great, and worthy, we get a greater
sense of accomplishment. Fulfilling some idea or plan of God is certainly noble enough. It fired up the Israelites to walk where no one
would have dared go before.

There is a difference, though, between public and private purpose in any vision for change and it is easy to confuse the two. While
we may have personal goals that are great and worthy, they may not
really involve the others we are trying to lead, and maybe they
shouldn't. Good leaders know the difference between working for a
common vision and for a personal one. Setting clear boundaries
between personal and public interests enables work to proceed
more smoothly and more easily. For example, imagine a high
bridge that spans a deep and dangerous chasm. Now imagine it
suddenly without any side-rails along the edges. You can bet that
cars will quickly slow down and hug the middle lanes. With rails,
however, they'll gladly go 60 mph, even right next to the edge.
Boundaries, like side-rails, enable faster work. Boundaries tell people where the limits are. A purpose, then, is rational, worthy, and
difficult, and it has clear public and private boundaries.

Second, we need to see and feel an emotional *picture* of the future with this change. What will my world be like with the accomplishment of this task? Pictures bring our emotions forward.
Pictures supply the fuel that fires feelings and emotions and moves
our personality forward as well. They provide the energy, the drive,
and the zeal to work, and to work hard. Images appeal to the
senses. For example, imagine a beautiful sunset at the beach. You
can, in a way, "see" the majestic colors cascade in your mind and the
whole image becomes captivating. Now imagine walking along that
long stretch of beach. Can you feel the sand on your feet? Can you
hear waves crashing on the shore and smell the salty sea breeze?
Does it make you feel peaceful and serene? Now imagine a fast-
moving train. Perhaps you "hear" in your mind the engine roar and
fade as it moves off into the distance. Does it make you feel adven-
turous? Or lonely? Or do you wish you were on board? Images like
these can evoke an experience from each of the senses.

The more the picture appeals to each sense, the more vivid and powerful its ability to move us. We can feel the experience of the Jews in Egypt by the powerful scenes the author used to describe their slavery. He then used a sensory image to help them dream of a better life. Moses brought vision, smell, taste, hunger, and pleasure into one memorable phrase: "a land flowing with milk and honey." Isaiah used the same power of imagery in describing the messianic age as a time when "the lion will lay down with the lamb." Imaginative and emotional pictures unite the passion of the heart with the purposes of the head. An emotional picture has fire in it.

Third, we must have a *plan* to get to this new place. If the people see that the leader has an idea of how to proceed, they are more likely to follow. Leaders feel more confident when they know where they are going, and so do the people. Of course, the more concrete and practical the plan is, the better. Nothing was more simple than for Moses to say, "Follow me!" Yet in today's parish the plan must be more detailed, and it must include provisions for feedback. After all, how will you know you are still on the right path?

The most often forgotten part of planning is to frequently give feedback on the correctness of the path taken. It is an essential ingredient for success. Moses did this by simply following the cloud and fire column (Ex 13:21) to stay on track toward the Promised Land, as well as by visiting the Lord in prayer. He continually readjusted his path by constant reference to the cloud and fire. We need the same process, although perhaps less dramatic. We will have much more to say on feedback in later chapters. In general, a plan gives direction to zeal, and feedback gives direction to the plan.

Finally, there must be a necessary *part* for everyone to perform. There must be solid participation by each person in the plan for it to succeed. In a successful parish no one works in a vacuum. No one should do meaningless activity either, for nothing saps energy more than the realization that what we are doing makes absolutely no difference to anyone! Every person must feel as if he or she is making a meaningful contribution to a worthy project, a project that does make a difference in the world. Each person must have a clearly defined activity to do that is essential to the success of the project.

Leaders must show beyond doubt and by actual behavior that they deeply believe in the new purpose and the plan to get there. They must show that they value each person as well. The leader's behavior is everything. No high-sounding words or brilliant plan will distract people from looking intently at the lived example of their leader. How you behave is crucial. That is why this whole program must be driven from the top. That example will reverberate throughout the organization for better or worse. We hope it is a good example. Changes can be driven from below, but it takes so much longer and is a much more chaotic process. Those leaders at the top who are skillful and lead by example will make the purpose, the picture, the plan, and the participation of everyone involved actually happen.

Together, these ideas provided the power that motivated the Israelites to move from slavery, suffering, and hardship to a completely new life in the Promised Land. Pushed from the past by pain and pulled toward the future by pictures of a beautiful dream of the way things could be, we can also move, change, and do meaningful work. Only these elements can overcome resistance to change. Only the right combination will unite leaders and workers in common cause. God used all of these elements through the words of Moses throughout the Exodus event. At each stage—at the Red Sea, at Sinai, and even upon entering the land—they were reminded of their *purpose* in vivid *pictures* and of God's *plan* for salvation and their *part* in it.

Communicating It All to the People

"Go and assemble the elders of Israel, and say to them..." (Ex 3:16). Right at the very start of the Exodus account, the Lord ensured that the purpose, picture, plan, and participation was communicated effectively to everyone. After all, the greatest mission in the world is meaningless if no one knows about it. Communicating the mission must be a constant concern. Leaders must make sure the message is transferred accurately and completely to *each and every* follower. There can be no time when someone does not know what is going on or what the issues are. Communication is the dynamic that builds connections between leaders and their followers. It cements their relationship. It helps create credibility in the leader and that trust and confidence that is so crucial to success.

What people would follow a person out into the desert if they did not really believe it was the Lord calling? The Lord helped Moses communicate the ideas about leaving Egypt in a manner that worked well. The Lord guided Moses throughout the Exodus events to ensure that his will was transferred to the people faithfully and constantly.

Of course, communication does not mean, "Now, hear this!" That may work in the Navy but it cannot work in parishes, especially for volunteers. There will be more on this in chapter 4.

Each of the four *p* words—purpose, picture, plan, and participation—has its own unique communication needs. Each one calls for a different technique or style of communication. Together, they ensure a complete, thorough program of leadership that is clear and effective. Almost every action of the Lord in the Exodus event included some provision for making sure all the Israelites either heard or saw it. Communicating with the people was a crucial part of getting everyone safely into the Promised Land.

Achieving Commitment, Control, and Change

Commitment, control, and change are the result of good communication and a good leader. Getting the purpose, picture, plan, and participation across to the people causes powerful forces to grow in the human spirit. They reveal something irreversible is happening in the organization, or in the whole parish. That alone can shake things up a bit. First, the four words strikingly reveal the leader's *commitment*. When someone goes to the trouble of setting up the dynamics of finding a purpose, painting a picture, and forming a plan for every person to participate in, everyone instantly understands the leader is committed. It is obvious that the leader is *involved* and has *serious* intentions. He or she is deeply involved in the project and is not easily distracted. This person has *thought* about it, *feels* deeply about it, and is willing to *act* on it. Moses prayed hard about his task, cried and wept about it, but ultimately acted on it. He approached the Pharaoh at great risk and spoke boldly about the plan. We are attracted to people who are committed and the four *p* words demonstrate an unmistakable seriousness about the future.

Second, they reveal simply that someone is in charge and that the situation is under control. They show that there is some significant person who believes there is something that *can* be done. While others might have done nothing for years, or spun harmlessly in circles with half measures, this leader has a real answer and will dedicate all his or her energy to it. This person feels *above* the problem, not struggling beneath it. This kind of leader simply believes the plan will work and is in a position to know so, either through special knowledge and training or just due to that unique perspective from above the problem. He or she believes that the problems affecting the parish are not insurmountable and that the plan is different from whatever has been tried before, if anything. There is a fundamental optimism to this kind of leader. This leader believes in the ultimate success of whatever project is involved and is focused on its completion. He or she knows the difference between a battle that can be won and one that cannot and marshals the group's efforts accordingly.

This control also has another important function. It ensures that any problem-people will be contained. There will always be those people who have other more obstructive plans, malicious intentions, or even malignant designs. These actions may be consciously deliberate or may arise from deeper unconscious layers of awareness. In either case they can be difficult to change or cure. However, they can be contained, so that their effects are muted. The four *p* words combine to produce an effective bulwark against those forces that derail the mission. We will see later how Moses used all four to counter the work of Aaron and the making of the Golden Calf at the foot of Mount Sinai.

Finally, the leader's commitment to the purpose and his or her power to direct events reveals the possibility of real *change*. Suddenly everyone realizes the future looks better. The people come to realize the leader may actually make a difference. That is a pretty exciting revelation, and it engenders one of the most powerful forces in the human spirit—*hope*. The chance that the future will bring what we deeply desire, have always wanted, and desperately need fires tremendous willpower to accomplish the goal. Hope makes the difference between a parish that is dying and one that is moving forward. Let's see how these words work in more detail now.

Chapter Two

Finding the Promised Land

Finding a Purpose

Sometimes a noble purpose jumps out and grabs us, shouting, "Do this!" Usually, as we know too well, it takes some time and work to discover. However, it is not enough just to find a good thing to do. It must be the right thing for *this* parish or group at *this* time with *these* particular people. All kinds of factors must combine to make sure a purpose matches the parish. Taking the time to find the right ones will pay off with success. Our goal is a single, long-range, energizing, and worthy purpose. The process starts with a careful search of the present situation.

Why must it be so careful and time-consuming? Unless there is an emergency requiring immediate attention, people tend to resist change if it happens quickly. There will be much more on this in chapter 5. How fast you act also depends on whether you are a new leader succeeding a strong or weak leader, or one considered effective or not. There will be much more on this in chapter 4.

Finding the right purpose begins with knowing where to look. Always look first among the people themselves. What is going on in their lives? What is happening in the neighborhood community that is on everyone's mind and in every conversation? What is at the forefront of their lives and instantly commands their attention? A wise leader will spend some time looking in various places for an effective purpose or noble mission, but the first place to look is precisely at the center of the lives of the people he or she hopes to lead. There might be important things going on there and the leader better know about them. The leader needs to know what is happening in the local news. What meaning does it have? For example, a big new shopping center development can mean either more money and opportunity, or more crime and congestion. What do the people think about it? What is happening in families right now? What is the economy doing locally? For example, does the rise of computers and office technology represent progress or threat? Do recent drug arrests mean new dangers for the children? The purpose must address those issues of import or else it will remain irrelevant. More specifically, a leader looks at those inner places within the human heart, precisely where those issues of pain, fear, dreams, and hope are stored.

What fueled the search for change among the Israelite people was pain. That is always a fertile place to look for purpose. After all, the first question doctors often ask their patients is, "Where does it hurt?" We can also start with that. Where in the organization or among the people is there discomfort? Where am I experiencing some difficulty? We can be sure every Israelite cried out for an end to slavery. They knew exactly where the pain was. Very often those are the immediate areas where God is inviting a closer and more thoughtful look. Even Jesus invited Peter to get out of the illusion of safety in the boat and meet him in, of all places, the windswept waves. Peter found Jesus in the storm. We can, too—precisely where we feel confusion, fear, and suffering. We can look to the pain in our life for ideas about new purpose.

Starting with pain is important. After all, if there is no dissatisfaction with the status quo, it is extremely difficult to convince anyone that a change is needed. For example, how many times have you heard, "What is so wrong with the way we're doing things now?" People like familiar things, and they don't change easily. You might describe a beautiful picture of a better future with great ideas and imagery, but unless there is some sense that the present situation is really awful, it will fall on deaf ears. No pain; no gain for your purpose.

Fears are a special type of pain, but then again, who likes to think about fears? Most people don't like to focus on what they fear. While pain tends to preoccupy, fear tends to remain hidden just beneath the surface. When frightening images come to mind, we tend to quickly move on to something else, and yet they are powerful motivators of human activity. As unpleasant as they are, fears are fertile ground for a vision and worth investigating. They just might pay off with a powerful goal. After all, Jesus led people through the ultimate fear—facing death itself—and discovered resurrection. We can, too. Fears can reveal what situation needs to change. For example, is the parish in a high-crime area? Are people afraid to come out at night? Is the economy in trouble? Are people afraid of losing their jobs? A good leader will find those fears that lie just beneath awareness and bring them up for a closer look.

We can also look to our dreams. If pain represents the awful reality of the present that we want to flee *from*, then dreams are the beautiful "promised land" of the future we would like to run *toward*. God speaks to us there as well. Thinking about our dreams and wishes for the future reveals a picture of life worth seeking. Our wishes, desires, and dreams are fertile ground for finding a purpose for change. Do you want more people to attend the parish? Do you want the programs to expand? Do you see a parish full of active and enthusiastic people? A good leader will find fast cooperation by asking for what the people already dream about.

Sometimes dreams are contaminated by fear. Dreams are more powerful when we can remove the fears, anxieties, and worries that accompany them and that have prevented the dream from being fulfilled already. Those terrible emotions stop us from moving forward. Ironically, people can be afraid of both failure and success at the same time. Failure makes them look stupid, while success creates high expectations. Fear of failure and success are unconscious roadblocks to change. A leader needs to know how to neutralize them. For example, a wise leader could ask, "What would you most like to accomplish *if you knew you could not fail?* What do you hope for, knowing there would be no failure?" Moses used both the awful present and a beautiful future to fire up his people to move, but he used the power of God demonstrated so visibly in the Ten Plagues to communicate inevitable success. When they felt that God's plan could not be stopped, they dared to dream of the Promised Land.

Leaders need to check their own hearts as well. They need to know what issues burn deep inside them; what fires their own imaginations; and what dreams energize them. Good leaders can bring each of these search actions to their own lives. After all, leaders cannot lead if they don't believe in the mission.

A final place to look for a powerful purpose is the directly stated visions of our faith. "Go and baptize all people." "That all may be one." "Love as I have loved you." These are divinely revealed truths and so already have much power precisely because they are rooted in our human nature as created by God. They are not "foreign" to our life but arise from where God placed them within us. Faith is not some imposition on our natural state. Faith *is* our natural state.

Pain, fears, dreams, and faith—these are the places we look for purpose. Although it is not fully formed yet, we know we are on the right track when it arises from all these areas. We will have more confidence that purpose will make a difference and change our group or even a whole parish tremendously.

Collaboration or Cooperation?

These two words are hot topics today, especially as more and more lay people assume positions of leadership in parishes. In the past a few priests and the pastor ran most parishes. Today, however, power is shared on a much wider basis. How clergy, religious, and lay staff work together is the subject of numerous workshops, seminars, and magazine articles. The words often used to describe these working relationships are *collaboration* and *cooperation*. Unfortunately, people use these words interchangeably, but they mean different things and describe very different realities. For the purpose of this book, I will understand them in the following way.

In *collaboration*, several people come together as a team and work on some project. The goals, methods, and planning of the project are determined by the group itself *as a group* rather than predetermined by a higher authority. Collaboration also implies a certain level of equality among team members. Although they might be handed an assignment from a higher authority and there might be different authority levels in the group, collaborators work more as a team. Power flows horizontally from person to person. While someone might technically be in charge, that person does not command the direction of the group. In a sense, the project itself is "in charge." Team members consider themselves in service to an idea, a goal, or a project. Whatever is good for the goal becomes the guiding principal that governs their process. They "work" for the project, not for a person.

Cooperation describes the participation of people in the goals, planning, and methods set by one person, usually the pastor or ministry leader. People cooperate when they agree to become involved in that person's activity. Whereas collaboration described a more "horizontal" style with power flowing equally back and forth among team members, cooperation implies a more "vertical" style with power and authority flowing from the top downward. This is not a bad thing nor is collaboration necessarily a good thing. Each has its appropriate setting and purpose.

Collaboration is useful at the start of things. The pastor might invite team members to "discover" a project together, saying, "Let's discover together the will of God for this parish. Right now, I don't know what that is. I know if we share our talents, ideas, and spirituality, we will discern God's will for us." Collaboration is the better process when the parish or ministry is starting a brand-new idea, like setting a five-year plan for the very first time. After the goal is set, then cooperation is the process used. The pastor or leader invites people saying, "Now that our purpose has been set together, let me invite everyone to come aboard and work with us together to make it happen."

Finding the Purpose Together: Collaboration

The most common mistake in leadership is leaving the people behind. Finding a purpose for everyone to accomplish means including everyone in the process of finding it. Like the Good Shepherd in the Gospel, real leaders must know their people well. We will talk more about the actual personality of leaders in chapter 4.

We leaders don't have to do all the work at finding a purpose. In fact, we shouldn't. That's good news. It means the responsibility for the mission is shared by those we hope to lead. The people should have something to say about where we are going. Sometimes the people will cry out for it without even being asked! That's the time to listen most intently. For example, a parish could divide all of its people into neighborhood guilds or groups. Each month the core staff of seven or eight key leaders could spend an evening listening to the people and their concerns. They could ask for both verbal and anonymous written comments covering the whole range of parish services and their needs. Care should be taken to record every idea so every parishioner's thinking is honored. Listening groups could be organized in other ways also, such as school parents, seniors, and newly registered families.

Listening carefully and skillfully to our parishioners can reveal where we need to go in a way that is more riveting than anything else. That might mean taking a survey or calling a meeting or simply getting a voice-mailbox. Good leaders notice what's going on among parishioners and listen to their concerns. Paying attention to them now can make a big difference later when it's time to move. People will follow those who respect them, and we show that respect by honoring their voices *before* we move. If we want them in the landing of the plane, we'd better include them in the takeoff. Why should we do that? We listen carefully precisely because we love our parishioners and know that God speaks through them.

Some leaders know the purpose instinctively. Call it inspiration, divine direction, or plain old good luck, they announce a mission for the people and hit the mark exactly. These leaders come along once in a while and instantly create a sensation. Maybe you are one of them. If not, this is a process that will produce the same results.

Forming a Purpose

So far, our process has identified *where* to look for a purpose. Now we want to begin *forming* it in a clear, concise, and compelling manner. We also want to make sure we have the correct purpose that truly speaks the needs of the people. At some point all these various ideas, forces, and needs must be articulated in one powerful message that is simple and easy to remember.

The first step is to collect all the people's ideas and suggestions. This can happen in a number of ways. A large group might require professional surveys or large meetings. A small group can use a familiar process called brainstorming. In brainstorming, a good leader invites everyone to speak their ideas. This means that they let their thoughts freely wander over a topic and, without any sense of censorship, speak all the ideas that spontaneously come to mind. This can be done for each category of pain, fears, hopes, and dreams. Within each category, the items are then prioritized according to some value, usually from the most important or pressing to the least. The value could also be cost, efficiency, or practicality. Brainstorming is an important process. Not every important idea is on the tip of our tongue. Brainstorming allows more ideas that perhaps might be unconscious or buried in forgetfulness to come forward, even those that might remain unexpressed for more simple reasons, such as embarrassment, politeness, or political correctness. Prioritizing helps us understand how we value them.

During the reflection, consultation, and brainstorming time with the people, the leader can begin to formulate a purpose in a few sentences or key ideas. A good way to begin writing a purpose sentence is to *keep the end result in mind*. What future situation, or event, or set of circumstances would resolve the pain in the group? What action would produce the dreams? What final situation would answer all the problems? What would solve the problem or produce the dream in a practical (or efficient, or costly) way? Keeping the end in mind keeps the purpose centered on all the issues the people have brought forward, and according to shared values. It makes sure that the purpose is actually addressing the hopes and dreams of the people.

Each sentence can take the generic form of a problem/answer sentence. For example, Moses could have formulated the Exodus event like this: *Pharaoh, let my people go! We will leave this life of slavery and humiliation, and return to our real dignity as free and chosen people of*

God. We will leave this foreign land of Egypt and return to our home in the Promised Land.

As each possible sentence is brought forward, the leader can ask if it addresses each opportunity and threat, fear and hope, or pain and dream, that surfaced during the reflection time. *How* it will do so is the topic for a later process. It is only important now to see *if* it addresses them. In the Exodus mission statement, Moses mentions both the physical and spiritual problems of slavery and the physical and spiritual goal of returning to the land and God. Notice how it met their deepest spiritual value. They would leave *together* and enter the Promised Land *together.* They were the People of God and as such, must act as one nation, "a light to the Gentiles." This purpose met their needs on a number of levels. This is the time for making sure the purpose is genuinely on target with the main issues and values of the people.

Keeping the Purpose Close to the People

Paying attention to what people are already feeling, saying, or doing may be the most important factor in developing a successful purpose. Remember that in the Exodus account God laid out a plan to Moses *in response* to the people's deeply felt prayers: "I have heard my people's cry and will rescue them" (Ex 3:7–8, 6:5). The mission to leave Egypt and return home resonated with the deepest-held beliefs *already* in the hearts of the people. This mission was no imposition of foreign or strange ideas. No Israelite heard these ideas for the first time. They were in their dreams every night. The power of God working through Moses was in realizing, capturing, and focusing the power already present in the wishes, dreams, and hopes of the people.

Skillful leaders can articulate those dreams especially well. When they do so, powerful psychological forces come into play. As people hear their own hopes and dreams proclaimed in the words of the leader, they are forged into a more closer bond with him or her. They feel more committed, closer, and more connected with what is going on. The leader and people walk as one and speak with a united voice. However, when ideas are heard for the first time, or in language and idioms that are foreign, the process of motivation is slowed considerably. The best speeches repeat the refrain already singing in the mind of the audience. Good leaders know how to tap into that song.

Getting to that genuine and authentic need is crucial. There is no point in wasting time solving the wrong problem. After all, the

Exodus wasn't about making better bricks or taller pyramids. That is why the prioritized list is important. If we choose too shallow a plan, or one with no backing, we will have no followers. God's plan was exactly on target with the real need of the people to return home. That mission physically and geographically expressed their deeper need to restore their human dignity as people created in the image of the free God. Finding a purpose cannot be done in isolation from the people we want to move. After all, leaders cannot really change others at will. They can only guide the changes people already want to make and need to make. The time a leader spends in thoughtful contemplation and careful consideration of what people are saying, feeling, and doing will reveal those needs more accurately and save a lot of time in damage control later.

A common mistake in leadership is to confuse a personal purpose with the public purpose. Leaders are often very talented, intelligent, and resourceful people. After all, they made it to the top, didn't they? It becomes very easy for them to feel convinced of their own infallibility. It becomes easy for them to feel as if their ideas are the most brilliant, cogent, and compelling ones voiced. The trappings of power, attending yes-men, and perhaps a docile congregation can all serve to strengthen this dangerous idea. These factors can beguile leaders into thinking they, and they alone, really know what is best for everyone; only they can set the course, only they can sail the ship. These leaders will soon be alone.

Does this mean that leaders are simply poll-watchers? Do they merely look for the prevailing winds of the shifting public mood? Of course not. However, the most effective purpose cannot ignore the crowd completely. The best purpose is one that *both* leaders and people support. It may mean that the leader thinks of it first, or articulates it better than anyone else, but the purpose cannot disregard the needs of the very people it is attempting to meet. How ironic to insist on a purpose to help people that they don't want! Leaders ignore the crowd at their peril. A careful reading of the Scriptures reveals that Jesus and the prophets expressed the deepest needs of the people in their teachings, even if they weren't consciously understood at first by the crowd.

What about a purpose that is only supported by the leader? Certainly there are those times when a prophetic leader calls for a change that is ahead of the awareness and knowledge of the crowd. A purpose supported *only* by the leader can still be accomplished. It is just much more difficult. It certainly means a lot more work for the one in charge. These are difficult situations to judge. After all, the leader is out on his or her own limb and, by definition, unassailable by common argument. Convinced of his or her own moral rightness, the leader will ignore any feedback or comments from the crowd.

These leaders attempt to move people in directions they alone feel are important. After all, they might believe that only they are high enough to see the "big picture" and know what is needed. That works for parent-child relationships, but rarely among adults. Remember, we were created equal in dignity before the Lord and one another so one person cannot arbitrarily rule over another. But the "brilliant" person will think he or she knows better. Ironically, very often these plans *are* brilliant! However, the goodness of the message is not enough. Even brilliantly crafted plans will fail if people are ignored. If people feel left out, they will walk out. If leaders leave the people behind, the people will leave them behind as they go off in their own directions. Real leaders take time to discover the underlying values that everyone can believe in.

Those leaders who have made their own brilliantly crafted purpose and have not included the people in the purpose-finding must then spend a great deal of time "selling" the idea to the people they hope to lead. They must convince those who are not part of the process how and why they should cooperate. The people must also examine the new "product," and all of this takes energy and time. If it doesn't work, the leader must start all over again. Worse still, the leader may become disillusioned or angry at the people for not accepting what he or she has worked on for so long. It is a tragic, misplaced, and wasteful anger. Worse still, that anger may inspire the use of force and coercion. In that case there is no leadership at all, just bullying.

Although a charismatic leader may succeed for a while by effective persuasion, or by force of personality, or simply by force, it usually doesn't last. Remember, compliance is not necessarily good leadership. Good leaders create followers who *want* to follow because they have *chosen* to do so. Followers who go along because of coercive manipulation or who are swept up in the charismatic personality of a star eventually grow weary of it. Their natural need to be treated as real human beings eventually surfaces. The leader cannot compete with that. Ultimately he or she is outnumbered and the crowd will sabotage the plan in almost imperceptible ways. It is very difficult to get people to go where they don't want to go.

How do we get that cooperation from people? One time-honored method is simply to be a good listener. That is a deeper concept than it sounds at first. We will hear about getting feedback throughout this book and more specifically in chapter 3, but listening, surveys, focus groups, and meetings are good places to begin. In fact, all of them are simply different forms of listening well to people. Although it is usually impossible to hear from everyone, there are valid and reliable scientific methods available that can accurately generalize to the whole group from the input of a few.

Another powerful tool is getting people to formally "sign on" to a project. For example, after announcing a new purpose, picture, plan, and participation program, the people could announce their acceptance of it. They could do so by signing their names to a document, standing up at a meeting, or even formally swearing their allegiance by oath. People do this at Mass when they say the Creed. Generally, the bigger the ceremony, the more powerful is the depth of commitment to the new mission. Moses actually conducted a little ceremony (Ex 24:7). The Covenant was read and the people accepted it by acclamation. This is especially effective when documentation is difficult. This was also a centerpiece of feudalism in medieval Europe when record keeping was minimal. The people swore their allegiance to a local lord, and the power of a promise kept was all that was needed. People actually do have an interior sense of personal integrity. Signing on–type events tap into the power of that dynamic. After all, people do not like to think of themselves in a bad way or as dishonorable. Good leaders can use that power to their advantage.

Another powerful tool that helps cooperation is rapid response. Whenever the people present some need, a rapid and effective response builds credibility immensely. People will tend to cooperate in the future with someone who honored their needs quickly in the past. People also tend to have an interior sense of gratitude. They are thankful for some gift. That is why merchants often hand out free samples as a good-will gesture. They know people will feel a sense of gratitude, or at least, indebtedness, and perhaps will buy from the company in the future. Good leaders who listen will gain cooperation if they respond quickly and effectively to what they've just heard. That does not mean they must solve the problem. Just a response is sometimes enough for the moment. For example, after conducting a survey, it would be a great idea to publish the results soon. That way the people can see that something happened with their responses right away and that it wasn't just an empty exercise.

Good leaders treat this whole process with a great deal of respect. After all, things are received in the manner in which they are given. If the whole process is performed in a very casual manner, then the input will be casual as well. The seriousness with which the leader treats the opinions of the followers will measure the depth and gravity of the response. People know when they are being taken seriously. No one likes their time to be wasted. For example, in the parish that conducted neighborhood listening sessions, the meetings should be announced as an important upcoming event at the Sunday Mass. Care should also be taken to set up the meeting well, with comfortable seating, refreshments, and a relaxed atmosphere. When people walk in the door, they should feel that this is a significant event. They should know that their comments will be recorded with their permission, and that these meetings will guide the direction of the whole parish.

Some leaders will try to manage the people's input. They may ask for opinions only in certain areas, thereby avoiding certain problem subjects. The first step in a real survey is to inquire about the people's needs and desires without any direction or editing from the top. Just let the people respond to whatever is on their minds. Of course, common themes may emerge and then the process of gathering and coalescing various strands can begin. However, even if only one common goal is discovered, it will more likely be the purpose and direction everyone will follow. They will recognize themselves in it because it resonates with the basic core values and beliefs of the people.

Keeping the Purpose Loyal to Core Values

Leaders can set a new purpose for any organization as long as they do not threaten *core values*. These are the virtues, the beliefs, the traditions that are most basic to the group. They are, as the name implies, the central identity of the organization. For example, a parish is formed from the value of following the Lord. It should not field an army to conquer other lands or join the New York Stock Exchange. Core values form the background understanding for the way things are. They define the main idea of what the "business" of the group is. It is a purpose that never changes even as new five-year plans are formed and reformed. Whenever a group wanders too far from these core values, it has truly lost its way. When people wander too far from their basic self-identity, they will often complain about "not feeling together" or "not feeling completely themselves." They aren't.

For example, we know the Israelites wanted a change from their terrible condition of slavery. They could not tolerate staying in

Egypt, but they would not tolerate leaving their God. Their core value or basic self-understanding was as "the chosen people of God." Other core values were "obedience to his word" and "faithfulness to the Lord." The changes Moses initiated respected those values; in fact, they fulfilled them. If he had said, "We will achieve our freedom by becoming better Egyptians and following their religion," that would have broken the Israelites' core values of loyalty to God. The people would have strongly resisted. People are more inclined to accept changes that respect their core beliefs. They will participate in the process if their basic identity is not violated.

For instance, in our parish listening-group example, it turns out that most of the parishioners happen to be college graduates and there is even a college nearby. They highly value education. Therefore this particular parish will have a core value concerning education. The people tell the pastor at the listening sessions that they want more resources dedicated to the parish school, adult education programs, and outreach to the nearby college campus. Growing in knowledge of the Lord is certainly a core value—our faith. It becomes practically expressed in this parish by the unique value people place on learning.

These core values are the guidelines that make sure any new purpose is coherent and consistent with the group's basic identity. They make sure that new changes are not just the whimsical idea of some dreamer. They also prevent the group from going off on wild tangents in areas far from their expertise. There are millions of wonderful things to do in the world, but not every one is the domain of every group. The Israelites did not decide, thankfully, to get into Egyptian religion. Each group has its core values and they must be respected, or leaders will become frustrated wondering why no one is following their wonderful ideas.

Closely connected to core values are *core activities*. These are the actions and behaviors that immediately flow from the core values. They are the basic "business" of the group. For example, a parish is about the business of realizing locally the mission of the whole Catholic Church, first and foremost. Groups must stick with what they are about. Imagine the resentment that might arise when, say, a parish liturgy group starts giving advice to the weekday bingo group. Each group has a core activity that is its reason for being. Each group must stick to its basic activity. It is extremely important to know it, publicize it, and follow it.

When change is coherent with these values and activities, people experience a kind of "click" in their minds that signals a resonance with who they are. The change seems right and acceptable. It does no violence to their sense of themselves as a group. By the way, this "click" must occur in leaders as well. They must also resonate with these same values or their leadership will be inauthentic. Leaders cannot lead against their basic principles. People will quickly sense their discomfort and they will rightly be accused of hypocrisy. When both leader and people share the same core understanding, there is a powerful harmony of feeling.

Ironically, these core values are often unexpressed. Even though they are the deepest-held beliefs for the group, most people could not name them right away. They exist as a kind of unseen and unexpressed "background" understanding of things. A very useful thing for leaders to do is to articulate in a simple and clear fashion these core values. There are a number of places to look for them. Leaders can look to the circumstances of the founding and origins of the group for insight into basic self-understanding. The parish's own history often reveals the basic core belief. Why was this parish founded? What has its history shown to be a consistent ethic? What does past behavior reveal? What has always been the main activity that no one else does exactly the same?

These questions go to the very heart of the enterprise that is ministry. They call us to reflect on the basic mission of ministers and the services they offer. If all the parish leaders understood precisely what they are offering people, they could focus their energy more closely on that service instead of becoming bogged down in side issues. No leader should worry about the amount of time spent in clarifying these core beliefs. Getting this down cold can prevent a lot of problems later. A few degrees off course is not a problem for a ship just a few miles offshore. However, a few thousand miles later, it will be in the wrong ocean!

Finding core values and behaviors is a soul-searching exercise. It calls for some thought and deep consideration. We are dealing here with the deepest values of a person; what makes them tick. We can look to our God-given human nature for some basic ideas, as well as the traditions of our faith. Real leaders take the time to answer these questions: What am I really about? What is the basic business or activity of this group *that no other group does*? What is *unique* about our way of fulfilling God's plan? What do I really believe in? These answers will keep the parish on track no matter where it "sails."

How do we know when we've arrived at a core value? It is not simple. We are dealing with things that are so basic and close to us that they are hard to distinguish. They are also very subjective.

However, our emotional connection can be a clue. Core values create *excitement*. They get our blood boiling. Because they resonate with our deepest feelings, we can actually feel the experience of arriving at a core value. If we produce a purpose that produces yawns, we need to try again. If we announce a goal that creates immediate volunteers, plans, and initiatives, we've hit paydirt. Core values also create willing involvement. When people really want to help, contribute, and cooperate with the purpose, we've probably hit a core value. Excitement and compliance are clues to a successful search for core values.

Pushing the Purpose to the Limit

But how much change is necessary? How far do we go? Change actually happens on two levels. The first level simply rearranges common elements. The second level changes the very category of the elements themselves. For example, on the *Titanic*, a first-level change merely shifts the deck chairs as the ship sinks. A second-level change involves taking a plane instead! Very often, first-level change is simply "more of the same, only slightly different." It is a cosmetic difference. Real change involves change on a much more radical level.

Only second-level changes can be big enough to excite people to become involved. We may get polite cooperation for leading first-level change, but cooperation does not involve people deeply enough and is just not satisfying. The Israelites were not invited to build better pyramids, or to be better slaves, but to change occupations completely. Only a second-level change is worthy of real, total, self-giving efforts, like daring to walk *through* the Red Sea, or to walk *on* water.

Creativity, imagination, and cleverness are the gifts that discover deeper second-level changes. Looking at situations from unexpected angles, different viewpoints, and unlikely perspectives helps find the insightful answer. Brainstorming, again, is a time-honored technique that invites people to express themselves without the constraints of logic, propriety, or even decorum. Ideas get thrown out in a crazy disorganized mix. Yet it is precisely that unorthodox juxtaposition of unlikely combinations that perhaps joins two ideas that would never have been associated before. Brainstorming first throws out disjointed words, arising from fears, dreams, and hopes. The words are joined in surprisingly different combinations to form phrases. Phrases then come together to make sentences and a nascent direction begins to form. That brings insight and second-level ideas for a vision of change.

Desire-define-decide-determine-discipline. This is a simple mnemonic device to describe the process of coming to and maintaining an effective purpose. We begin, of course, with *desire* either for or against something. Whether it is our own idea of what needs to be done or the people's, no purpose will last without a burning sense of urgency. It must be something we *really* want! The purpose must have strong feelings behind it or it will fade away. That is why a broad base of support is so important. That is why leaders must speak from the hearts of their people. *Everyone* must feel strongly about it. *Defining* the issues simply makes things clear, especially for those outside the experience. It clarifies the core reasons and beliefs for those who perhaps don't know about the situation that gave rise to the burning issue in the first place. *Deciding* on the purpose starts the work and gets things going. It is the starting gun. It reveals that oscillation is over, indecision is past, and a course has been set. It is time to move forward. *Determination* describes our attitude toward the move. We will not be easily discouraged or dissuaded from the chosen path because there is a lot of courage and power behind the decision. *Discipline* simply means we are focused. No other task, obligation, or issue will distract us from the plan. We have a schedule and it will be followed. Rules and guidelines are in place and there is an accepted procedure that will guide us to the finish. These five ideas are just another set of words to help in remembering the essential points about purpose and vision building.

Staying Focused on the Purpose

Fire and smoke kept the Israelites on track. There could be no mistaking the direction to travel with a huge column of fire at night and a pillar of smoke by day marking the way. They were visible for miles and therefore they were visible to *everyone* in the caravan. If Moses had even tried to steer a new path, he would have had thousands of voices correcting him. The people must have been grateful for such a beacon. After all, they were not exactly desert folk anymore, and the way must have been difficult to find in a trackless, arid wasteland. Thank heaven, truly, for the fire and smoke.

The signals also served a more affectionate purpose as well. They signaled the continuing care and attention of the Lord. The columns of fire and smoke kept the Egyptians, and any other desert marauders, at a safe distance. This towering natural wonder kept the power and care of the Lord literally before the Israelites' eyes.

So it must be with any leader's purpose today. It must be before the people at all times in some highly visible way. Leaders can use banners, logos, letters, speeches, events, and celebrations to keep the purpose visible. Attention spans vary, but they are generally short, and wise leaders plan on some or all of these continual reminders of why the path is in this direction. They not only then signal a sincere and strong intent to complete the mission, but also their care and attention for the people. Guiding leaders offer continual reminders of their ability to stay focused on the goal.

This is more easily said than done. Distractions are many. While some distractions may be natural and unavoidable, others can be more deliberate and even malicious. For example, if there is some economic crisis in the country, or weather disaster, or even a sudden illness of someone on the staff, plans will be affected. But sometimes the crisis is man-made for the very purpose of derailing the mission. People may try to overload the system with too much data and then demand a thorough analysis before proceeding. Some will put forth objection after objection, demanding almost total perfection in all things before agreeing to move. Some will continually offer alternative after alternative to investigate, always delaying the decision to move until every possible scenario is discovered. More will be said on these ideas in chapter 5, but real leaders generally stay focused on the purpose and do not allow themselves to be side-tracked.

Here is a simple technique that can help keep you on track. Sometimes during meetings or other events, the activities of the event or the dynamics of the conversation itself can sweep us along the wrong path without even realizing it. Wise leaders mentally stop themselves for a moment, and in their imagination, rise above the room, turn around, and look at the situation as if they were another person. This is a powerful imaginative technique. While in this "above the room" position, ask this question, "What is going on right now?" Continue to ask this question periodically throughout the event. The question means simply this, What is actually being discussed or done at this moment? Is this the right thing to be doing? Is it worthwhile? Do I want to continue participating in it? Positive answers confirm continued involvement. Negative answers call for some action, like making a change, calling the attention of the host, or perhaps even ending involvement.

A second important technique for keeping on track is to frequently measure the awareness people have about where the group is going. Just stop someone in your parish or organization and ask them about the purpose, the plan, or their participation in it. Do they know what the purpose is? Do they know what the ultimate goals are? Leaders should never just assume their followers know any of these things. Wise leaders frequently check to make sure.

Is there ever a time when plans should be delayed or changed? How do we know whether some new information is merely distracting or is actually vital new data that demands flexibility in our mission? This is an important distinction. Some new information can be crucial and a minor adjustment here or there just might avert a disaster. How can we tell the difference? First, we can ask, "Does the new information violate one of our core values? Does it compromise a core issue that is central to our identity? Does it threaten the core ethos of the group?" Second, we can ask, "How much of a change does this new information demand? Is this a second-level change, or merely a first-level change?"

Once the leader sees that core values are not in jeopardy and only first-level changes are involved, he or she can ask a few more questions: "How much of a delay will it cause? What is the depth of support for it? Does only one person want this, or many?" For example, if it represents a simple cosmetic change that several people want, and it only affects the appearance or surface qualities of the purpose, then a wise leader can allow it.

Making the Purpose Effective

What makes a purpose a powerful force for change? Simply put, an effective purpose creates its own energy. A powerful purpose instantly brings to life a vision of the future that connects with everyone. These visions resonate in our soul. People instantly recognize them as important, needed, and vital. They have an automatic connection with life because they come from God, who is the author of life. They speak to the central concerns people have been expressing in their hopes, fears, and dreams. We know we have struck paydirt if we hear comments from people like "Of course!" and better still, "Let me help!" We know we really hit paydirt when people say, "I can't wait to get started!" All really appropriate and powerful mission statements have the same qualities. They are short, instantly clear, challenging, and exciting. Just the naming of the goal generates enthusiasm. They literally create their own energy and motivation.

People do not become distracted with strong missions. If a person is told he has cancer, you can bet that his prayer to God about that illness will be intense, focused, and undistracted! Cancer is the central thing in his life and he is *very* interested in it. We pay attention to those things most pressing on us. If our prayer is about central issues, we won't get distracted. If we pray about little things, our minds will wander. In the same way, the mission we present as leaders must address the central burning issues of our people or they will easily become distracted.

One way to ensure we have a central issue that resonates with a lot of people is to weight the issues. For example, in the listening-group parish, the people could be divided into smaller groups. During a large meeting, many comments and ideas surface in a chaotic manner and it is difficult to get a direction. In each small group, however, seven or eight issues surface. Each person votes for his or her favorite three issues, and the group tallies the results to determine its top three. Then all the groups compare and tally the top three issues for the whole evening. Similar issues are combined in acceptable ways, and slowly a consensus emerges. There are several methods for weighting issues, and it is important to do so. A parish cannot set off in a direction based on an idea that one person found interesting.

For example, in that evening's listening session, people were talking about a new church that had just moved into the community. It had a very active proselytizing effort and was making inroads into this church. Parents were concerned about losing their children and adults were concerned that they didn't have the answers they needed to respond to the proselytizers. Slowly, a common thread emerged among individuals and across the small groups: this church's members needed to grow in practical knowledge of their faith, to make the liturgy more compelling, and to make the whole parish experience more hospitable and welcoming. A purpose began to coalesce around the three issues of hospitality, liturgy, and education. These ideas will be effective because they address the main issue going on in the minds of the people in this church. They will be excited about working on these ideas.

We can recognize an ineffective purpose by its complexity. If it takes a lot of explanation, requires special understanding or education, or worse, has intricate and elaborate structures, it will excite no one. On the other hand, if the idea simply restates the obvious it will energize no one. If the purpose needs a large, sophisticated marketing campaign to "sell" the idea to the people, then we probably have the wrong plan for change. If it meets strong resistance, it may have offended something very basic to the people and their organizations. It may have offended core values. If it meets a lackluster ho-hum response, it may only be addressing first-level changes that no cares about. These purposes are very common and simply reveal a lack of effort to discover the ones that work.

Finally, we can put these ideas together and develop a single sentence that defines the direction, the path, the goal, and the destination of our journey. It can be in the form of a sentence that contains the following parts: it addresses who will accomplish the goal, for whom it will be done, what and how it will happen, and why it will be done. We can simply fill in the blanks of this generic sentence:

> Our purpose is to serve _____ with these activities / events / products, in order to accomplish _____. We will do this by _____. We do this because _____.

If Moses were to fill in these blanks he might write something like this:

> Our purpose is to serve the Lord by freeing the people of Israel from their slavery in Egypt, to accomplish the restoration of their rightful place as a "Light to the Nations." We will do this by leading them immediately out of Egypt and back into their own homeland. We do this because it is the will of the Lord.

A few questions can begin our thinking toward discovering a noble and worthwhile purpose that is worth our best efforts.

Questions for Reflecting on the Purpose

1. What would I like to accomplish if I knew I could not possibly fail?
2. What are my hopes, dreams, and wishes for the future of my workplace?
3. What are the biggest problems around here?
4. Why do I believe we are not on the right path now?
5. What do I need in my personal life to be more successful?
6. What three things need to change the most in my workplace?
7. What do I need from the office staff to be more successful?
8. What have I heard from our people about what is needed here?
9. What do I think is going on spiritually with the people?
10. What is the one service I can provide that is unique?
11. What can I do that will make a significant contribution to the parish?
12. What simple title would I give this vision?

Painting the Picture

Imagination is crucial throughout this whole experience. Having a picture in our minds of our future life keeps us fired up and energized for work. The power of the imagination is awesome. Keeping a picture in our heads of the desired state of affairs or the goal we want organizes our mental resources effectively. Although there is a tremendous wealth of new scientific data that supports this notion of imaginative power, athletes have known for years that visualizing the sporting event for which they are preparing somehow marshals their physical and mental resources in a coherent way that achieves the desired result. Psychologists call this exercise neurolinguistic programming. Athletes call it visualization. Most people call it imagination.

Ironically, what fires something so ethereal as imagination is the body's very real and concrete five senses. Imagery that appeals to the senses makes any picture especially vivid and memorable. The more the idea is associated with specific sensory experience, the more powerful it becomes. For example, the phrase "a land flowing with milk and honey" includes some excellent sensory images. Creamy cow's milk and thick golden honey are both liquids with vivid colors and textures. The image of them flowing is so out of the ordinary in an arid desert that it is almost absurd. Yet that absurdity makes it stand out even more. If auditory or olfactory sensory images had been included, the image would be even more compelling. Such images would implant themselves even more deeply in the imagination of the people.

The image needs to be implanted deeply. We need the vision planted deeply because ordinary life experience tends to work against the staying power of ideas, especially in hard times. A purpose, even a noble one, will fade with the passage of time, especially after a few difficult events. A purpose built only on logic will fade with the first storm. A good solid picture can change a fair-weather supporter to a faithful one. That well-drawn picture can keep everyone on track. The emotional, physical, and sensory picture creates the most lasting effect.

Television and advertising media in general use this technique of targeting imagery for each sense to make lasting impressions on consumers. The media have developed it to a high art. After all, consumers go to the store long after they've seen the commercial on TV, so products need a picture that *retains* its staying power in consciousness for some time. There will be moments when we cannot think clearly, when the task seems too difficult, when the goal just seems too far away. Emotional images can carry us over these tough times by revving up our feelings and energy to a higher pitch.

Sometimes a new purpose is coupled with a unique ceremony that especially fixes the experience in memory. Weddings, baptisms, and ordinations are emotional ceremonies that speak of underlying commitments and display elaborate public rituals. Each ceremony includes elements, such as incense, candles, and songs, that address each sense. In these highly visible and sensory ways each public ritual serves to separate life *before* from life *after*. The more powerful, public, and emotional the ceremony, the more lasting its effects.

Moses, speaking for the Lord, called all the Israelites to engage in an elaborate ritual the night before leaving Egypt. The public family ritual of sacrificing a lamb, sprinkling its blood on the doorpost, and eating a specially prepared and unique meal embedded in the minds of the people that this night was different from all other nights and that they were about to engage in something incredibly important and unique. We can only imagine the emotions they felt as they packed to leave the misery of slavery forever. The Scripture is evocative: rough leather sandals, just-baked unleavened bread, the sound of thousands singing prayers. We can only imagine their joy in knowing that God remembered them and that they were going home. The imagery of that first Seder meal remained deep in their consciousness for centuries.

The story was told for centuries by fathers of families responding to the simple question of their children, "Father, why is this night different from all other nights?" Telling stories is a technique that especially involves imagery. A story that includes people with real emotions and colorful images can move us even more than any single image can. An effective story is a whole succession of sensory-laden images. The story does not necessarily have to be a complete narrative either. Martin Luther King Jr.'s famous "I Have a Dream" speech was a series of evocative images of children of many races and backgrounds playing together. Jesus described the kingdom of God using typical scenes of farm or city life: "The kingdom is like a farmer who went out to sow...." When leaders want to paint a picture for the people about the place they would like to take them, they will succeed with that kind of evocative imagery in story. Listing statistics, facts, and numbers is informative but not really very moving. People may nod in agreement at the correctness of the numbers, at the logic of the argument, but not get fired up to do anything about it. A story involves listeners in a narrative in which they can recognize themselves. Since their own life is a continuing dramatic story in which they are vitally interested, presenting the vision in a story form will more quickly appeal to them.

Certain stories are more compelling than others, of course. These narratives describe certain basic outlines of the most common situations and are very familiar. After all, there are only so many situations people can experience in relationships, and these stories fall into a set number of categories or "archetypes," as psychologist Carl Jung called them. They have been repeated so often throughout human history that they form an enduring pattern. These stories address basic issues of survival, pleasure, and personal significance or meaning. They are just naturally more compelling. In a way, these archetypes form a set of "templates" on the brain that are ready-made to recognize any new story or event that has a similar character or pattern. Those new stories with the same set of characteristics will receive a more attentive hearing or capture the audience's attention more easily. We are more "primed" to resonate with an archetypal story.

In addition to the archetypal *narrative* content of a story, its *emotional* content is important as well. There is physiological rationale for this idea. The area of the brain that processes emotions is primordial, predating in evolutionary time the development of the cerebral cortex which contains the areas of higher logical thought processes. This primordial brain system is more directly tied to ordering bodily functions. Emotions are simply ideas that arouse these physiological reactions. They are thoughts we *feel* in our body and were the first experiences our early brain processed. For example, certain external data, like seeing a saber-toothed tiger, caused our early ancestors to run, fight, tremble, or at least get a little excited. A quick connection to physical response was important to our evolutionary success.

The cerebral cortex did not replace these earlier, more elemental brain areas that process emotions but developed in addition to them. However, neural impulses still pass through the more primordial part of the brain before they are processed in the cortex. Neural stimuli that trigger these primordial needs and arouse a physical response are the most powerful emotions. Over the thousands and thousands of years of modern human development, certain common life experiences with heavy emotional content tend to repeat themselves. For example, meeting a friend or an enemy, feeling hunger, enjoying safety, or sensing danger are common emotional experiences for all people in every age and in every place. They have the power to capture attention.

If today we receive any new sensory information that matches these common archetypal emotional criteria, we might experience the neural information as something frightening, joyful, or saddening as well. That will deeply color how the cortex receives this new information, even if at first glance it doesn't seem like an emotional message at all. Any message that resonates with those needs will capture our attention quickly and deeply. For example, a politician who announces "Support the oil depletion tax!" will likely be met with yawns from most people. If she translates her message to something like "Support my tax and make money!" she will attract more attention. In our culture money instantly translates to survival and joy—strong emotional forces. This message gets home quickly. Mission statements that easily translate into these emotional templates that address such basic human emotional needs are more effective than those that simply state logical ends.

Describing the Picture Now

Even though we want to change the present situation, we need to make sure we know exactly why we are leaving! Painting a picture of the present also helps fire the desire to move. Anything that channels energy to the goal is important. A vivid image of what has been tolerated so far reminds everyone how necessary it is to go through this whole process. Every time Moses referred to the people making bricks without straw, he was painting an image of suffering and endurance under an intolerable Pharaoh. It was an effective summary of the years of abuse they had received at the hands of a brutal regime. It was a clear reminder that their situation could only get worse. It was time to leave. It was time to go to the Promised Land.

We can determine just what this picture is in the same manner that we discovered our purpose. First, we brainstorm all the experiences of the people about the present situation. What are the present strengths, talents, and blessings we have now? What is going well? Where are we strong? In other words, what is good about our present circumstance? This is helpful to know because we can build on what is already going well as we reach for our future goal. There is no need to throw everything out. Next, we brainstorm the present weaknesses. This may produce results that are similar to those produced by the purpose-forming process. There is always a certain amount of overlap when we take a long careful look at any group of people such as a parish. However, the purpose-forming session focused more on some desired future state, while here we are look-ing only at what is right before our eyes. After brainstorming all the strengths and weaknesses, we can then prioritize the list according to importance.

Questions for Reflecting on the Picture of the Future

The first four questions ask for the foundations behind the basic services we provide. Number five is very subjective but definitely implies there is always some way for improvement. The next two bring in sensory impressions, and the last two ask for personal impressions.

1. What benefit will this vision have for the people?

2. Why would they want this vision of the future?

3. What is unique about it?

4. Does anybody else provide a similar service?

5. How can it be improved?

6. What words describing this vision appeal to each sense?

7. Is there a single picture that captures the essence of the vision?

8. Is this vision worthy of our best efforts?

9. What story would capture this picture?

Chapter Three

Getting Started on the Journey

Planning the Journey

Now that our purpose is set and we have a picture of the new place in our mind, we need to determine how to get there. Planning is the road map to our purpose. It is the mechanics of success, the nuts and bolts of achievement. Moses put some thought into the Exodus. It was not a whim or sudden impulse. He made plans for it, and so must we if we hope to arrive in the new "promised land" as he did.

Purpose, mission, and vision are the titles we use for the overall direction we set. They describe the largest picture, and it should be simple and focused. Goals are the next level down. We usually set several goals that taken together will produce a single purpose. Objectives, the next level down, are the several sequential steps needed to reach the goals. Tactics, the next level down again, enable us to reach objectives. These terms are just some of the leading and motivating jargon we often hear today. While each has a classic definition and describes a unique aspect of planning, they all involve one similar dynamic. They are all about keeping an eye on some future event and working to make it happen. *Planning* deals with the actual process of work itself. In *purpose* and *picture* we set the course and painted the scene; now we set out the steps to get there. This is the work part.

Plan on planning. Expect it. Depend on it. It will save a lot of work later. Planning our work means laying out all the steps we need to take before we begin. It involves anticipation and a certain amount of fortune telling. We have to guess the future. We have to guess that these steps will get us where we want to go. It is better to look ahead before marching than after the march has begun.

Chinese wisdom teaches that the longest journey begins with the first step. The purpose laid out in our vision for the future is by nature a long-range mission. Because it is a large, worthy, and noble task that is difficult to accomplish, it will not be done quickly or soon. There are many smaller goals to meet along the way. The first step is to divide the mission into these smaller goals. Some of these goals may have already been revealed in the prioritized lists made in the last chapter. While the mission or purpose is over-riding, long range, and large, goals are more immediate, short range, and smaller. Objectives are even smaller still and represent those activities that accomplish our goals. Tactics are smaller yet and represent most activities. Always though, goals, objectives, and tactics must clearly point to the purpose. At no point should anyone say, "Why are we doing this activity?"

Goal setting and planning are some of the most written about dynamics in organizational life today. There are many planning schemes and programs around, such as Management by Objectives, the Deming 14-Point Method, and Total Quality Management. But just setting goals and planning per se can never be enough. Certainly how they are set is important, so the leadership and motivation ideas already presented here will be key elements in the plan.

Before Setting Goals

We need to take a snapshot of the present situation in a way that is more informative than the pictorial one from the preceding chapter. We can easily do that by looking again at all the ideas that came forward during the brainstorming session. All those ideas about fears and dreams can be organized in another way to reveal where we are right now. That will help us set our goals more easily and accurately.

Simply put, we need to know four things about our present situation: its strengths, its weaknesses, the opportunities, and the threats (SWOT). These four items are similar to the categories we used in finding a purpose. Strengths are those aspects of the group that are working well. They may be people, programs, or things. We are proud of them. Weaknesses are those areas that need improvement and still need attention. Strengths and weaknesses are about the inside of our parish. Opportunities and threats are external; they are conditions that represent possibilities to exploit or dangers to avoid. Opportunities usually represent a future event such as a coming population shift or economic change. Threats are the opposite; they are elements of concern. Whatever or whoever is capable of preventing or hindering the direction we want to go is a threat.

Moses quickly went through this SWOT process at the very beginning of his mission from the Lord (Ex 4:1–17). He recognized his weaknesses in his slow speech and inarticulate manner. He acknowledged a threat in the possibility that the people may not believe his encounter at the burning bush. Both were real problems that Moses brought to the Lord's attention. There would be no point in going forward if these items were not addressed right away. The Lord reminded him of his strength, symbolized by the powerful staff, and of an opportunity represented by the eloquent and talented Aaron. Immediately after this talk, Moses had the confidence to tell his father-in-law, Jethro, that he was going back to Egypt to carry out the Lord's will. A little planning does wonders for the sense of confidence we need to do something great.

In our parish example, the newspaper announced huge changes in the way government welfare monies would be distributed. The pastor considered this an important event; it was either an opportunity or a threat. He called a parish committee together consisting of social workers, businesspeople, and lawyers to investigate the new changes and the possible impact on the community. The committee felt that there would be a significant interim period before the new welfare system would be effective. In the meantime there would be a significant increase in the number of people coming to the parish for assistance. The shift to a new system would cause great confusion for those needing assistance and parishioners might also be confused about the proper and right way of helping the poor. The potential for class division between rich and poor and general political strife was real. The parish needed skilled people and a program for meeting the problem.

The committee also made a list of the parish's strengths and weaknesses in meeting this issue. The nearby college meant access to experts in the field for adult education programs. The student body could also provide a huge pool of generally idealistic young people eager to work for justice for the poor. Since the local business and corporate community was concerned about a rising homeless population in the business district, they could contribute the services of their lawyers to help with legal issues. This committee helped the parish a great deal by anticipating a problem and quickly understanding the resources available to meet it. The committee ensured that the parish purpose was going to deal with an actual important future event that would be on everyone's mind soon. They ensured the parish goals were realistic and effective.

This pre-goal-setting exercise is important precisely because it establishes the available resources and gives advance warning of possible problems. It prevents going in the wrong direction. For example, the pastor would have been foolish to plan for a major capital campaign at a time when the town's main employer was about to close down, adding to the problems caused by the welfare changes.

Forming Goals by Planning Smartly

Goals, objectives, and tactics will need to be planned at each level of purpose. Because the purpose is now set, we will talk about goal planning in this section. The best leaders plan in a smart way. In fact, by taking the letters of the words *plan smart* we can see an easy way to remember what to do. We remember the *p*urpose, to *l*ist priorities, to *a*ct on those priorities, and to do it *n*ow. Moreover, the individual goals must be *s*pecific, *m*easurable, *a*ttainable, *r*elevant, and *t*imed.

First, we must always remind ourselves of the *purpose*. Our goals must be clearly related to the purpose. They should obviously connect to our goal in the "promised land." Upon hearing the best goals, people should respond, "Of course! That is just what is needed!" In other words, these goals are obvious and have a lot of immediate support. For example, if the pastor announced an adult education program on social justice for the poor, everyone would know this is to address the threat to the parish of the new welfare program changes. Everyone would know it was part of the overall effort to grow in faith, make liturgy compelling, and improve hospitality. Even though that threefold purpose grew out of the experience of the proselytizing church coming to town, the new adult education program also fits the purpose.

Next, as in the last chapter, we again *list* priorities in a freewheeling brainstorming session. We want to get as many ideas out as we can without regard to practicality. This frees the creative process to be innovative and perhaps to discover spontaneously the one novel idea no one has thought of so far. After writing these diverse goals down, we can go back and prioritize them according to appropriate and practical considerations.

Then, we resolve to *act* on these goals. In leadership, behavior is everything. Leaders lead by initiating and following through on some action. Something actually happens that is different. Action is the lifeblood of leadership. Inaction drains the group of life and spirit. Any purpose that remains in the realm of theory or idea will disappear through lack of interest. Parishes around the world are littered with mountains of paperwork outlining great five-year plans that remain firmly ensconced on the shelf. That only increases cynicism among the staff about planning in the future. Planning means action.

The willingness to act is actually a measure of the correctness of the goal or purpose. Willingness to act measures how compelling the purpose is. If there is no excitement to act, if there is no urgency to begin, if people are not fired up at the starting line, then the purpose was wrong. Goals cannot simply be nice things to do. They must be connected to the people's deepest concerns, issues, and needs. People will become excited about those issues. If the purpose is right, just the name will fire up tremendous energy to start. For example, if you have just been diagnosed with cancer, you will not be very interested in petty goals about better lawn care or carpet stain removal, but you might find goals about health care suddenly fascinating. In the same sense, leaving Egypt immediately struck every Israelite with enthusiasm for the journey. Using straw to make better bricks did not.

Finally, we resolve to act *now* on the first goal. Acting now not only means progress, it also reduces stress. One of the main sources of stress is unfulfilled expectations or unfinished business that remains "hanging over our heads." Acting on the project gives a sense of accomplishment, movement, and progress, a sense that we are actually doing something.

Most goals are long range and cannot be accomplished quickly. They will remain hanging over our heads for some time. However, if we do something every day toward the goal, we can still feel the sense of movement and progress. It is very important not only to schedule a beginning to the work that day *but also an end.* Dividing the day clearly into "on" and "off" working periods frees the mind to concentrate when it needs to and to relax completely at other times. This prevents thoughts of unfinished business from intruding on the time when the mind truly needs to rest and recreate. Many leaders find themselves consumed with thoughts about work all the time, which leads to great stress. They might feel guilty that they are not working on the project even late at night. Acting now, and knowing when to stop acting, reduces stress and accomplishes even difficult, long-range goals more easily.

This finishes the first word, *plan*, in our acronym, *plan smart*. Our second word is *smart*.

A goal should be *specific*. The more concrete and practical it is, the better. It usually takes a little trial and error to hone a goal down to its concrete form. After all, it probably starts out as a vague wish or dream that contains several ideas. Each goal should have only one point and should be expressed in everyday language. For example, "We want to increase church revenue by 10 percent each year," or "We want to leave Egypt, now!" Our parish example might say, "We want one class a week devoted to adult Scripture education."

One way of ensuring specificity is that it is easily *measurable*. This is the area most often forgotten in goal setting. *There must be a way to determine clearly and quickly whether the goal has actually been met.* Goals need some kind of clear feedback mechanism to determine success. We simply need to know when the job might be over, or how far we have still to go. Quantifiable goals are easier to measure than qualitative ones. For example, if your goal is to increase revenue, you can easily check the bank statement and determine success or not. You can check the calendar to see if adult education classes are scheduled. If your goal is to become nicer, that is much harder to measure.

Goals should be *attainable*. For example, maybe I will have to finally admit that I am not going to make the NBA all-star team this year (or any year!). That is hardly a real or attainable goal. We need to be reasonable when we set out to accomplish something. "Large and worthy" does not mean large and impossible. This is a judgment call by the leader. Obviously what one person calls unattainable, another may call bold and visionary. An extraordinary, bold, visionary, second-level plan becomes attainable with a detailed plan that outlines clear *intermediate* steps. If each step is attainable, then so is the final goal. People must be able to feel they can really make it. They must really want it, as well.

Goals should be *relevant*. Simply put, let's keep to our own business. We need to ask if these goals are really in our line of work in the first place. Relevant means we should stick to our own business of the Gospel. Goals are relevant, or *valid*, when their content concerns genuine ministry issues. *It means we have to spend some time making sure we know just what the concerns and issues of our ministry are.* For example, starting the Renew Program is in our faith area of concern, while starting a commercial business is not. Everyone must agree on our concern areas as well.

Finally, goals should be *timed*. They should have some calendar date connected to them at which time we determine if it was accomplished or not. For example, if you set out to make a million dollars by age thirty, you have a specific date to check if you made it or not. Trying to be a "good" tennis player "sometime" leaves you unclear about how well you are doing or when you have arrived.

Shaping the Plan

There are several areas to consider in shaping a plan. These ideas can help a parish committee focus their efforts in the right way. For example, one parish felt there wasn't enough active participation at Mass. They decided to begin a new effort to enhance participation. Well, the Mass is a big topic so they needed to determine first what exactly the *product* was that they wanted to get across. It may sound funny to speak of the Mass as a product and there is certainly no intent to be disrespectful to the center of our worship. But the idea here is evangelization and that is taking an idea or experience of one person and getting it across to another. We are simply calling the experience of one a "product" to be "transported," if you will, to another. This parish decided to break the Mass into several key ideas: the Liturgy of the Word, the Liturgy of the Eucharist, communion, and the power of singing and music.

Second, this parish plan could establish the *placement* of the services or actions. If the vision is worthy and beneficial, then the people need to be able to receive it easily. They need to be able to "get at it." God placed at the service of his people in the desert a fiery column and a pillar of smoke to guide their way, as well as food and water. He made it easy for the people to feel his attention and care. The business world calls this customer service. We call it "loving our parishioners." We love them enough to look after their needs in a way that is beneficial for them.

For example, if this new adult education program is started, it will need to be at a location and time actually convenient for people to show up! If a new evangelization program is started to canvass a neighborhood, it will need to be done when people are home. If a fund-raising drive is started, it will have to be made clear to the people how to participate. If the vision is to spread the Gospel, it must be done in a way that people will hear it. How the vision is placed before the people is an important area to set goals.

This particular parish decided to place the program at Mass itself. For four Sundays the homily period would be used for catechesis on each of the four key ideas. Of course, it was announced that this was a special temporary circumstance, which the *General Instruction of the Roman Missal* allows. At the end of the four weeks, the parish would also distribute a booklet at Mass containing a printout of the whole series so everyone would have a record of the event. It could be given to people who did not attend as well.

Third, the vision needs to be *promoted.* The best ideas fly by themselves, but some will have to be explained and actively promoted just to distinguish them from the barrage of information people receive every day. Sometimes it is difficult to rise above the din of constant information overload. Moses correctly expressed a concern that he alone would not have enough credibility to make the people believe he could effect their rescue. He needed the credibility of the God who was the God of Abraham, Jacob, and Isaac. He needed help promoting the idea of exodus.

Promotion can simply mean connecting with people. It means creating an opportunity when both leader and people are on the same wavelength. Once heard, the vision must be powerful enough to create its own interest. Of course, the intensity of feelings shown by leaders about the issue is a huge factor in getting it heard, but it all doesn't rest on their shoulders. A plan should include ideas about advertising and persuasion. Promotion is the part that deals directly with resistance. Knowing the reasons for resistance to change can help in crafting a response that will ensure effective promotion.

For example, one way of highlighting a new program is by stopping the old ones. Not having something draws attention to what is happening. The committee could recommend that other programs postpone events until after the four-week liturgy program. This is out of the ordinary and would stand out among the general advertising overstimulation people receive. That is good promotion.

Another form of promotion is a large banner. In the parish liturgy-education example, the committee decided to include a large banner at the front of the church to remind people what would happen at the homily that Sunday. In that highly public location they thought it might also attract nonpracticing members driving by to perhaps stop in. They might be intrigued at the notion of a little instruction in a service whose meaning they had long ago forgotten.

Finally, the plan must include provisions for cost or *price.* This doesn't automatically mean money, although clearly that is the most common cost to pay. It could also mean the price in physical work, time, disruption of present habits, personality change required, or general efforts extended to make this plan a reality. If the price does mean money, then it should be thoroughly explained, rigorously simple, and logically complete. Money is a very powerful psychological symbol. People feel very strongly about its management, or lack thereof. There can be no ambiguity about how the people's money is used. There can be no secrecy, so be aboveboard with finances. A good plan respects the power of money.

The parish liturgy project had very low overhead. It involved the cost of a banner and the booklets, as well as the loss of only four weeks of Scripture-based homilies. The price was reasonable and affordable. It would give the final go-ahead to begin the series on liturgy at Mass.

Questions for Reflecting on the Plan

1. What business are we in when we do ministry?
2. What is the product or service we will provide in this vision or goal?
3. What are the three main things we want to accomplish?
4. How will our people receive this service?
5. Does our plan reveal that we genuinely love our parishioners?
6. How do we plan on promoting the service?
7. How much will it cost? How will we pay for it?
8. What are the main problems with this plan?

Participating in the Purpose

No one we lead should ever wonder, "What should I be doing around here?" Ambiguity about work roles is a proven cause of stress and is destructive to that sense of participation we want. Aimless activity is debilitating and gradually erodes the spirit. If people are not certain about their role, they will lose interest and, worse still, lower their standards of behavior. All these reasons indicate how important participation is to getting to the "promised land," for it involves the people's actual activity as well as the leader's attitude toward them. It involves the people's sense of their own importance, worth, and significance. Everyone must feel that importance. People will not participate for very long if they don't have some sense that what they are doing is important and connected to the efforts of the rest.

Each person must have a clear idea of what the task is, why it needs to be done, and how important it is. Even though a person's task may appear to be peripheral to the final goal, that worker must know how that task actually relates to the goal. Every person must feel a part of something larger than the assigned task and must know precisely how he or she is helping to achieve a goal; otherwise, that worker's interest in participating will be lost. In a well-run organization, one with any hope of arriving in a "promised land," people must know what, and why, they are doing what they do.

For example, we all know how debilitating people find assembly-line work. Turning one screw on a machine for hours is boring and meaningless, but so is blocking linemen on a football team. There the actions are obviously integral to team success, even as mudslogging as they are. Prior to the game you can be sure the coach diagrammed the play on a locker room chalkboard and made sure everyone knew what to do. The coach's circles and *x*'s clearly indicated the play *would not work* unless each person performed his task well. Every part was related to another. People can perform astonishingly difficult jobs if they believe it is important and needed by their teammates.

Every person in the group becomes a *hologram* of the whole picture. Holograms are those remarkable high-tech pictures made with laser photography. They produce amazing 3-D images on flat clear panes of glass. Yet even if the glass is broken into tiny pieces, each individual piece retains the image of the *whole picture*! Each piece contains complete information about the whole. Each person in the group must also know the purpose, must have been involved in forming the purpose, and must know how his or her work contributes to it.

Communication in the group helps that happen. Isolated workers know nothing of what others are doing. Disconnected workers may become a problem. They may start out simply ineffective, yet can easily become dangerous. Isolation breeds resentment, and then a feeling of devaluation. Resentful workers sometimes seek revenge. If each person could talk to everyone else, the sense of connectedness would increase. Good leaders provide those opportunities. Good parishes allow and encourage that kind of communication. Most parishes have a lot of organizations. Each person in the group must have a system that enables clear two-way communication with the leaders not only of that group but of other groups as well. Weekly meetings, monthly roundtables, newsletters, e-mail, Internet home pages, bulletin boards (both electronic and physical), memos, speeches, and discussion groups are various methods that can help. Occasional special ceremonies that reward or acknowledge different groups or people also powerfully remind everyone what and who is important. Combining all of them in a clever matrix is the best method.

This helps in a number of ways. Not only does it release the workers' creative ideas, it also enables each person to see, hear, and benefit from shared wisdom. It also enables the leader to gauge the mood and concerns of the staff. Best of all, it allows the leader to communicate changes, encouragement, or new ideas quickly and effectively. Communication creates a sense of team. The best team includes members who know what they are doing, and why.

Revealing the Natural Desire to Excel

Deep within every person is a natural desire to do well, to succeed, and to excel. If that desire is nourished, the person can truly do great things. This is an important point that reveals why the other four elements actually work. People *want* to do well. It is naturally embedded in the human personality. On the other hand, *how* to do well must be learned. While we may want to excel instinctively, the way to do things is *not* instinctive and we need to be taught.

Even little children eagerly "study" their parents because they want to imitate them and become as effective in their own little world as the adults are in theirs. Children want to *do* things and to do them by themselves. They beam with joy when they first ride a bicycle or throw a ball or just stand on their own two feet. If God hadn't placed in us the impulse for accomplishment, we would still be crawling around on all fours. Once we know some skill or action, we develop an automatic desire to succeed in it. If given the chance, the training, and an opportunity, people will rise to the occasion because they *want* to be effective.

The key to motivation is in tapping that naturally embedded desire to do well in a noble and worthy work. The key concepts of purpose, picture, plan, and participation provide the opportunity to channel that powerful drive for excellence into a helpful church-oriented direction. Why not use it for the work of the Lord? Doing the will of God is certainly a big enough task; it transcends our needs and is the best motivator of all.

That desire can be frustrated by a lack of direction from above. When people find themselves in meaningless work, when they see no real consequences of their efforts, and when they don't even know how well they're doing, that desire for excellence dies. Good leaders must see to all those issues.

Using Good Feedback to Correct Our Mistakes

Accomplishing a difficult task is satisfying, but it rarely happens without a few mistakes along the way. Sometimes we won't even know we've made them. Ironically, people have a deep need to know these failings, as long as the process is private. A person likes to know, "How am I doing? Does my work measure up? How does my work compare with everyone else's? Just how do I stand in the world? Am I doing this work right?" Feedback from a trusted and knowledgeable person adds tremendously to success. This is an important point and, again, probably the most frequently missing aspect of work situations. Of course, feedback cannot be autocratic or doctrinaire, and public feedback can be dangerously embarrassing. It is difficult to do well. People work best *when they are in control of their own feedback*. When the standards are so clear and so well known that workers can see quickly for themselves where they stand, then self-correction occurs and success follows.

For example, while riding a bike, the mind is constantly getting feedback on balance and speed. You naturally make adjustments to both. Knowing that the alternative is a painful crash means you get better quickly! Constant feedback that occurs during the action is the key point. The mind uses feedback in a very effective dialectic to improve skills rapidly. Of course, skillful direction from a boss can also help, if it is given privately in the manner of a good encouraging coach or a friend who is on the side of the worker. Good leaders nurture the natural desire of people to improve their skills with good and frequent feedback.

While bike-riding feedback is almost unconsciously done, mental feedback should be more thoughtful and deliberate. Once again, the practice of mentally rising above the situation, turning around, and looking at the event from "above" is an excellent habit that improves objectivity. From that imaginary perch we can ask ourselves, "What is going on here? Is this the direction I want to go? Do I want to participate further in this activity?" These questions recalibrate all of our instruments back to the purpose. They reset the course. Better to do that sooner rather than later.

Imagine a boat setting out for Hawaii. The crew looks forward to a great vacation and all eyes are on the horizon. A charted course that is a few degrees off just outside the harbor is not a problem, but a few thousand miles away means they will not reach Hawaii. Everyone needs course corrections. The more frequent, the better.

Sometimes we don't want to rely on intuition or on empathy or on reading minds to know what our people are feeling or thinking. We can ask them directly and listen to their concerns. How wonderful if we could do that with every person. Real leaders will try to follow the example of Jesus the Good Shepherd, who knew his sheep and his sheep knew him (Jn 10:14). Jesus was the shepherd for whom "not one of them was lost" (Jn 17:12). The leader who can talk and listen to every follower is lucky. For most, it is impossible.

Sometimes speaking with just a few can suffice, if it is done correctly. There are valid, reliable scientific methods that can take the comments of a small number of people and generalize them to the whole population. A whole science has developed around the use of these very useful exercises called focus groups. This is a scientific method for statistically guessing the opinions of large groups by measuring the responses of a representative smaller group. When done well, focus groups can be very informative.

A survey method is *reliable* when it produces similar results each time. It is *valid* when it actually measures what it says it is measuring. Both aspects are important. However, a trained professional is needed to develop the surveys correctly. Since many important decisions follow from these responses, it is well worth the effort. The creation of valid, reliable questions and the analysis of people's responses are a complex science, but extremely powerful and effective.

Formal feedback methods can include all these techniques: focus groups, surveys, questionnaires, and meetings. The purpose is the same in each case: to hear from the people. Each method usually directs the person's attention to some specific area of ministry. For example, "What do you think about our new adult education program?" However, it is also important to include the opportunity for generalized input that may not be anticipated. We can simply ask, "What else would you like to say?" While we might want information in one area, we may not be aware of problems in another. If given the chance, people will tell us. Giving people the chance to speak on whatever comes to mind allows us to discover those unexpected areas of concern that might have escaped our attention. It also shows our respect for the opinions and needs of our people.

Finally, wise leaders will examine the feedback from their followers to assess themselves as communicators. It is not enough to give a speech; we must find out how much, if anything, the people *actually heard and retained*. Have we been able to communicate the purpose, picture, plan, and participation dynamics to the people? How much do they know and understand? Does the feedback indicate that the people know what is going on in the organization? Is their knowledge compartmentalized to just their own section, or are they aware of the larger effort of the other groups within the organization? No matter what the leader finds out, it is good news. It is good news because now, at least, he or she will know the truth. The leader can either rejoice at the good efforts or know right away where quick improvement is needed. The only failure is not to know at all. That kind of disconnection from the people is disastrous.

Creating the Desire to Participate

How do we create the desire among people for participation in the purpose? How do we create a sense of "ownership" for the parish? The answer lies within that important relationship between the leader and the people. Certain dynamics will create a bond of loyalty that translates into participation. Basically, a good leader will *support* the people in good times and *train* them in the tools they need to succeed in bad times, *acknowledging* their ideas, opinions, and suggestions and *rewarding* them when they do succeed. Support, training, acknowledgment, and rewards help create that loyal bond that produces a sense of ownership and participation. Let's look at each of these ideas.

Support is needed at moments when a work situation is not clear. Confusion and unrest happens so people need to feel the leader's support. Simple images can help. For example, when Moses presented the powerful picture of a "land flowing with milk and honey," the people used that picture in moments of confusion to help focus their attention on the purpose of their leaving Egypt. There will be times when the vision looks too far away, or the reasons for the work seem blurry, or there is a sudden change in the working conditions. Having a personal picture helps remind us who we are and what we should be doing. For example, the traditional Latin phrase, *alter Christus*, "other Christ," is a simple two-word description of the role of a Christian leader. It simply means "be like Christ in every situation." At times when it is hard to think straight, it can give form to a foggy sense of self and the work to be done. People will then see their leaders have remained focused and steady in spite of the confusion. Supportive leaders can also provide simple, clear pictures of each person's role in the purpose.

Regular one-on-one meetings also instill a powerful sense of support. Supportive leaders schedule regular meetings, one-on-one, with every person on the staff. Most parish teams have regular staff meetings. However, those are group events and not everything can be communicated effectively in a group setting. Sometimes staff members are intimidated by group events. Sometimes a leader can say much more in a private setting. It is reassuring for everyone involved, especially in very busy parishes, to know that he or she will have time with the leader. The staff member knows every week there will be guaranteed private time with the leader to clear the air if there are any concerns, or if issues are not addressed at the larger meetings.

Support also includes all the ideas of communication discussed earlier. Knowledge is power, and the more information people have the better. They need information to do their jobs and to know how the whole group is doing. Of course, secrecy is important, as are all issues that require confidentiality. However, it is often overused by insecure leaders as a veil to hide their lack of skill. When leaders trust their people with ample information, they build trust. The people feel supported, trusted, and valued. They feel a sense of *inclusion*, and that builds the sense of team and ownership even more strongly.

Another subtle form of support is good old-fashioned etiquette. Interrupting, shouting, rudeness, and ill-mannered behavior are forms of abuse. They actually signal a lack of respect and disregard for a person's dignity. Civility in language, politeness in manner, and a natural gentleness in the way we talk helps convey a sense of support for the personal dignity and value of each person there.

Training simply means helping people do their jobs. It means teaching the skills they need. People are more inclined to participate if they feel they will be trained. It is often a missed opportunity in many organizations. Lack of training is presumptuous. It presumes there is nothing left to learn, or that skills learned years ago have remained perfectly honed. That can hardly be the case. We can always improve in abilities no matter where we are now. Good leaders continuously provide training opportunities for their people.

Training is not difficult. In fact, it should be simple. First, the trainer identifies a standard to be met. The trainer gives as clear an idea as possible about what is expected. Then, if possible, she actually demonstrates the action. Next, the employee or worker is invited to try it. Mistakes are common at this point, so the trainer can adjust the procedure and give valuable feedback to the employee. Remember that helpful, encouraging, and coachlike feedback is one of the most powerful tools for modulating human behavior. Finally, as the person improves in skill the trainer lavishes praise on him, but only when there is actual improvement. Good trainers know that praise

without accomplishment or accomplishment without praise is coun-
terproductive. Good self-esteem comes from both. Training is an
opportunity to *do* both.

Acknowledge the input of the people. Leaders must acknowledge
their people in two ways. First, leaders must be sure that everyone is
involved. No one can feel left out or unimportant. Active, real, and
practical participation by everyone on the team is crucial to success.
If any one person sloughs off, it greatly reduces everyone else's
morale. Second, leaders must make sure that each person has an
important part to play that *captures his or her interest*. If it doesn't,
they both can seek some way of adapting, changing, or reinventing
the position so that it does.

One powerful yet simple tool that enhances ownership is simply
asking people for advice, counsel, or answers. People feel honored
to be sought out for input. They feel respected for their intelligence
and ability. They will feel loyal to a leader who has consulted with
them and that motivates participation. This can happen both formally, as we have explored before with surveys and meetings, and
informally. For example, when passing a worker in the hallway, the
leader can stop and request a quick opinion. That kind of casual
request for the person's input communicates that the person is important, needed, and valued for his or her intelligence and abilities.
Everyone likes that and people respond by caring about the program. They feel as if they are "part-owners" of the project. That motivates participation.

Another important form of acknowledgment is showing interest
in the staff members' personal lives. Sometimes leaders forget that
their staff members have lives outside the church. They might have
children enrolled in sports, or scouting, or other interesting programs. They might be involved in interesting charities or volunteer
efforts. Expressing an interest in those activities is a more personal
form of acknowledgment that makes people feel as if they are
viewed as more fully rounded individuals. For example, the leader
might inquire simply, "How did your daughter do in the soccer
game last week?" or "How is your grandfather feeling after the
operation?" Workers will feel as if the leader cares about them as
persons, not just as workers doing a job. This acknowledgment
brings a humanness to the relationship between leaders and people.
The leader knows that the church is not the entire world of the staff.
However, the usual care must be taken that appropriate boundaries
are not crossed. Interest cannot grow into intrusion or interference.

Rewards are those moments when people receive some positive feedback on their work. Although the actual work done may be quite varied and diverse, everyone can offer some kind of feedback on the process itself. Feedback is immensely important to self-understanding. Accomplishing things is central to our sense of self-esteem and we need to know how we are doing from objective sources. The closer the feedback is to the actual work done, the better. Performance appraisals that come at the end of the year can cause more harm than good because they are just too far removed from events. We can even tolerate negative reports better if they are immediate. It means we might be able to adjust our performance in time to try again right away.

Finally, the feedback must be related to the purposes for which the work is done. Obviously, personal grudges or anger cannot be a part of it. People can usually tell if they are being treated fairly and objectively. Comments must be related to helping the work accomplish the group's purpose and not some personal revenge by the leader. Feedback rewards may be positive or negative, but if they are timely, accurate, and fair they will improve conditions quickly. Remember, people want feedback and when it is done well, they will use it eagerly to improve their performance. When we offer suggestions, comments, or critiques on ongoing activity, we help shift responsibility for the project to the whole group. Everyone is then looking for the answer to make things better. Besides, who knows more about the actual process than the people on the front lines who are closest to the work.

We cannot take motivation for granted. Good leaders know this and never intentionally frustrate the most important resource they have in their followers—the desire to do well. How do leaders create participation? Supporting people, training them for the tasks they will do, acknowledging their input, and rewarding them for it are important key components of participation in the plan that will achieve our purpose. Good leaders never take their people for granted.

Questions for Reflecting on Participation

1. What is my real job description around here?

2. What are the top five tasks I actually accomplish here?

3. Is everyone doing something he or she considers worthwhile?

4. What is a simple phrase that quickly describes my role here?

5. What do I really like to do more than anything else
   in ministry?

6. What task is the most difficult for me to finish?

7. Can I learn more about the tasks I will do for the plan?

8. How can the tasks be best improved for the future?

9. Have I sought all the possible training opportunities?

Communicating with Credibility

Nothing happens in leadership without good communication. No leader can lead without connecting in some way with the people. Simply put, that is communication—the veins and arteries of a parish. It is all the connections that happen between a leader and the people. Communication transfers what is in the heart and mind of the leader to all those who follow. It may involve simple acts like speaking to a group or privately to each individual. It may involve writing letters, or making large signs, or websites on the Internet, or any one of a host of creative and imaginative techniques. After developing a great purpose, picture, plan, and participation, a wise leader uses whatever communication dynamic is appropriate to get the ideas across. However, there are some things which must be communicated first.

Of course, the very first thing to communicate is authority, or the very right to lead and be in charge. For Moses, that right came directly and somewhat miraculously from God at the scene of the burning bush. There God conveyed to Moses the authority and the competence to accomplish what was said would happen. Simply put, God communicated credibility. Moses then had to communicate to the people his connection with the Lord. Just as the Lord had to show his authority and power to Moses, so Moses had to accomplish the same thing with the Israelites. His opening move needed to be remarkable and memorable. After all, Moses was attempting to start something new. He needed to get their the attention. They needed to know that something special, new, and interesting was about to happen. Moses knew that and complained, "What if they do not listen to me?"

Just how do we get people's attention? It is not easy. People tend to be preoccupied much of the time, and with good reason. Life is difficult and people have a lot of concerns throughout the day. Usually, they are concerned about those things, people, or events closest to their heart, such as family, friends, home, and job. People also tend to want their situation to improve. Actually, they show a great deal of responsibility by thinking about how they can improve the lot of any of these things. Any topic that will address that need will usually get their attention, but only if done carefully. The goodness of the message is not enough by itself. It must be presented in a certain way.

For example, imagine you are sitting alone in your home late at night. Perhaps you are a little afraid and have a large heavy flashlight with you. Suddenly, someone comes crashing through your front door and runs quickly over to you. The shock of the crash might frighten you so much you hit the person over the head with flashlight, only to find out it was a panicked neighbor rushing over to report their house was on fire. That is an important message, but crashing into a house may produce a drastic reaction. Well, a person is like a home. If we want to engage another's mind, if we want their attention, we had better take careful steps to enter that home respectfully. If we barge in too suddenly, we will get resistance, no matter how important we think the message is.

Breaking through the cloud of distractions and preoccupation and the general swirl of thoughts inside a person's head is the first task of any communicator. It is not easy to do. Some leaders think speaking loud works well. Others think barking orders gets results. It does, but perhaps not the right kind. Shouting may get *compliance* from people, but that is not leadership. A person could shout commands all day and still not be a leader. Remember, a real leader creates a *voluntary* desire to follow.

Of course, a miracle or two always helps. In the Exodus account, Moses used remarkable signs—a staff changing into a snake and a quick-healing leprous hand—to convince the people that God was involved. But which God? This was a polytheistic time and people acknowledged many gods throughout the region. Once again, communicating the right idea at the right time was crucial. God was revealed as the same God their ancestors worshipped: the God of Abraham, Isaac, and Jacob. This greatly established the credibility of both Moses and the Lord with the people. The God of their ancestors was already credible and had proved to be worthy of belief through various signs and great deeds. God was right in communicating that quickly. Moses was right in asking for it.

What was that worthiness? What made God credible? It was care and love. The people knew God had already shown a deep caring for them. They knew God had their best interests at heart. He was on their side. That is the kind of leader people *want* to follow. They liked this God who came forward when they needed Him. They wanted to follow the same God who had sustained their ancestors. Connection with an established authority certainly speeds up the process of acceptance, but just a legal or juridical right is not enough for real leadership. People connect more with someone who will provide for their needs. They will look kindly on anyone else who can do the same. If everyone likes a certain pastor, leader, or minister, then showing a connection with that person can help you realize the same acceptance. Otherwise, you will have to gain it on your own.

Moses now had the attention of the people. Next, he had to actually communicate something and that was a problem. He was not articulate (Ex 4:10). Of course, the Lord would help him improve, but at the beginning God enlisted Aaron to be the first public spokesperson because he was more polished. That is an important lesson. Effectiveness is the goal, and it must be accomplished. God shows a practical nature here. He uses the best means at hand to get the idea across. Just because a person has a certain title does not automatically mean he or she is talented in every area. Better to choose people for tasks based on their proven skills rather than on their titles or status. This story reveals the creative side of communicating. Of course, it was a clever idea to use Aaron, but sometimes we can even find better communicators than people. Today, there are all kinds of options, from video, to newsletters, to websites, to skywriting! Good leaders think about that kind of effectiveness. What will get the idea across *in the best possible way*? What is stopping it now? The Lord would not let Moses' lack of skill deter an important mission—the mission of salvation.

Exodus 4:18–26 reveals another subtle but important quality that Moses possessed. He returned to his father-in-law, Jethro, and tied up all the loose ends from his former life. Moses made sure he had no obligations to his former life before he took on the new one. A leader must be free to perform the tasks required. There should not be anyone waiting to kill you either (v. 19)! Moses had originally fled into Midian to escape mortal danger. Moreover, there cannot be anything the people can point to that will mitigate authority, credibility, or trust in the leader. By asking for permission to leave Midian, Moses honored Jethro—a very important thing to do among Semitic peoples. If Moses had started this project, only to have someone find out later he had dishonored his father-in-law, he would have had an uphill battle to restore the people's confidence.

This is a subtle, very short section of Exodus, but it is an important one. Moses ensured he could communicate with credibility.

Moses' first act of communication was to talk to the elders (Ex 4:29). By getting the already accepted elders onboard, Moses greatly shortened the time needed to spread his message with good credibility. Going over the elders' heads directly to the people is also an option, but it is much more risky. If you are lucky and score a huge hit with the people on your first speech to the crowd, you might intimidate or win over the elders. But if you don't, you will have resentful and influential elders sowing resistance behind your back. Moses spoke to the already proven leaders first and established his authority, credibility, and trust with them immediately. Aaron, of course, actually did the talking.

Through Aaron, Moses communicated the main message of concern and liberation offered by the Lord. It had an immediate effect and the people were moved. That word *moved*, of course, refers to the feelings of the people. We use it here to signal a deep change in mood, but it is almost a metaphor for the message itself, which was to move out of Egypt and into Canaan. The Israelites knew right away they would be moving to a new place and that is what leadership is all about. The words leaders communicate should always reveal a direction and a destination.

This pattern of establishing authority and credibility, effectively using already proven elders, and setting direction is repeated many times throughout the story. These dynamics become constant concerns for leaders because people's confidence tends to fade easily, especially in the face of a crisis. We know there were a lot of those moments in the story! Moses repeatedly had to reestablish everything. However, he always returned to the same process because it worked. After all, they eventually made it to the Promised Land.

Putting It All Together in a Story

Purpose, picture, plan, and participation are the four key words that will get us to the "promised land." They worked for Moses and they will work for us. There is a fundamental logic to their order as well. First, the purpose sets the direction. Then, the picture fires the will to do the work. The plan sets out the order of events, and participation assigns the individual and group tasks. The "head" is in charge of the whole process. The "heart" provides emotional power to fuel the work. Next, the plan gives a method, and our part to play makes the whole project personal and meaningful. Most important, the leader communicates the whole story in a way that is clear, confident, and credible.

For example, imagine a new pastor arrives in a parish that lies in a tough part of town. Perhaps it is an area of high crime and low wages. The former pastor had basically given up on the place years earlier and had been simply marking time to retirement. The new pastor and associate arrive about the same time, but know little of the place. The staff is small and used to the old pastor's quiet ways. The people attend church dutifully, seemingly content to "pray, pay, and obey."

After a few frustrating months, the pastor is wondering what, if anything, is possible. One night, there is a drive-by shooting in front of the church. A child, a parishioner, is killed in the crossfire. The community is saddened by the crime, but they are also outraged. The pastor recognizes there is a real pain felt deeply by everyone. He senses the people's frustration and knows they have no place to express it. He knows the frustration will smolder into bitter resentment if left un-addressed. Crime is everywhere and the people are fed up. Like the Israelites in Egypt, they feel oppressed by an insurmountable force.

The pastor calls a meeting of a few respected people in the parish. He asks for their thoughts and opinions, and receives a strong sense that something has to change. Those who attend the meeting feel honored to be included and sincerely want to help. On the next Sunday, the pastor asks the people from the pulpit to speak their thoughts about their community. He invites them to call or to write him during the week. However, only a few respond. After all, this was never done before and the people don't know how serious he is. He knows, though, that crime is the foremost issue. On the following Sunday, he declares that the parish will fight crime and that he will take the lead. He openly challenges the local gang toughs to put down their weapons, to end the violence now, and to come to church. He asks everyone to come to a meeting in the church during the week.

No one has ever seen that boldness before! More people come to the next meeting, if only to see the man who spoke so courageously at Mass. He challenges the people to speak as well, but only in the safety of the parish hall. He values their input, so he chooses someone to record all the comments. The pastor summarizes each comment and checks it for accuracy with the speaker. Over and over, he hears stories of anger, frustration, and fear. Crime has lowered the value of property and has forced employers to relocate.

Later in the week, he calls meetings of each parish organization and asks for their input as well. The larger leadership staff meets with various community experts such as the police, sociologists, psychologists, lawyers, and job counselors. Finally, the pastor sends a letter to every parishioner who could not make the meeting asking for ideas and thoughts. The message comes through loud and clear from the people. Crime causes fear, panic, and lost jobs. The message from the pastor is also emerging in the minds of the people: change is possible.

The pastor next announces a month of prayer and reflection. Special services are organized to ask the blessings of the Lord and the wisdom to know His will in this endeavor. People continue to offer prayers, ideas, concerns, and suggestions. The original first committee of respected parishioners begins organizing the input into a coherent picture of parish intentions. At the final service, the pastor announces the *purpose* of the parish for the year. Every parishioner will work toward making the whole city virtually crime free by taking seriously the commitment to live the example of the Lord. It a spiritual purpose. The pastor quotes the beautiful *picture* of Matthew 5:15. This parish will be a lamp set on a stand, whose light will shine on everyone in the city. It will be a place where everyone can walk in the cool of the evening without fear. It will be a place of open doors, open factories, and open hearts. It will be place where children grow up, and grow up healthy. The parishioners *plan* to meet in small and large groups throughout the year for education in civic issues, application of Gospel ideas, and discussion of ways to reach resolution. They will learn and then act. Finally, every person will *participate* and be responsible not only for his or her own family's nonviolence and healthy growth but for the neighbor's as well.

The people are organized by blocks into neighborhood groups. At weekly meetings they socialize and come to know each other. Each meeting has a scriptural and prayer section, then there is education from various sources (the police department, social workers, employment counselors, psychologists, and religious teachers). Finally, there is ample time for discussion and resolution making. Each group makes a report of their activities and progress. These reports are shared with the pastor and the other groups. Each group is educated in knowing and caring about their community and about each other. It is all done in the context of growing in faith.

Each person first accepts the responsibility of knowing his or her own family situation well, using the information learned in the groups as well as the positive and loving encouragement received from the other group members to help the family become nonviolent and crime free. Each person accepts responsibility for helping the rest of the group also. Finally, each group accepts responsibility for how the other groups are doing, so the whole parish is working together.

On a monthly basis, the leaders of each group meet with the leadership staff to share progress, concerns, and decisions. The pastor sees to it that the purpose is maintained. Every three months, there is parishwide renewal at Mass to reaffirm positive progress and excite new interest from new members. Every six months, there is a parishwide rally to reaffirm excitement, hope, and energy. Every meeting includes a recommitment to the Lord to follow his will.

Everything is geared to the purpose. Major financial decisions are made in the light of that purpose. All parish activities are geared to it as well. School lessons, religious education sessions, retreats, Sunday sermons—all make use of the themes of fighting crime. For example, school activities use role-play, classes, and lessons on non-violence, conflict resolution, and safety. Adult education stresses job skills, financial planning, and parental discipline. All classes and activities use Scripture and tradition to ensure that the whole effort is spiritual. The purpose must be, and must be seen as, fulfilling the will of the Lord.

This story is only imaginary. It follows most, but not all, of the ideas presented here. No situation can make use of everything. Each parish will have unique circumstances that will mean unique applications of these ideas. Generally, the four key words are an effective way to capture, galvanize, and organize the passion of the people to accomplish something grand, noble, and beautiful. All of our work can be as a "light set on a stand, where it provides direction to everyone in the house."

Chapter Four

Staying in Charge of the Journey

Taking Bold First Steps on the Road

The journey to accomplish the purpose could be a long one, so it had better start well. The road to the Promised Land for Moses and the Israelites wrapped around the entire Sinai peninsula; it took forty years and a whole generation to accomplish. We hope that our purpose will not take as long, but it will always begin with a first step. It had better be a bold one.

The first actions we take are crucial to success because everyone will look to see where this new direction is leading. These first impressions are difficult to change later. The best first impression to make is a bold one that says it will no longer be business as usual. There must be a strong message that something new and powerful is happening. The first steps must galvanize opinion and grab attention. Because of people's natural resistance to change and their love of the familiar, this first step must be riveting and startling enough to capture their interest. However, boldness does not mean brashness or bluntness. Sometimes *gentleness* is bold, especially when contrasted with a former leader's harsher manner. Jesus was a strong and bold, but not harsh, contrast to the hypocrisy of the Pharisees, who laid burdens on others they themselves would not carry (Lk 11:46).

What that bold step is depends on whether you are a new arrival on the scene or have been promoted from within the parish. If you are brand-new, you will need to take some time to get to know the situation before making any changes. Rapid change by an outsider comes across as arrogant. "After all," people will say, "you barely know the place and you think you have a better way." Rapid change is insulting; it says the people were too dumb to recognize these changes were needed before you arrived. What you need most at the beginning is more information, not a new program. Still, some bold step is needed. A powerful first step could be to announce a process of parishioner feedback. Let everyone know their feelings and opinions are important and you will take the time to survey them. That boldness will make a very good impression and signal that you honor the people you will lead.

If you arrive at leadership from within the organization, ministry, or diocese, it might be a better idea to accomplish something sooner. Since you are already familiar with the situation you can make changes with more credibility. However, you will need to establish yourself as your own person and not a protégé of the old administration. A bold change will signal that you are in command and ready to go.

How do you make a bold gesture? Sometimes it can be done by *not* doing something, by cutting something out of the schedule, by focusing efforts on one simple idea. Letting go of several policies, procedures, or schedules sends a signal that the leader is serious about this purpose. Sacrifice is an age-old sign of commitment. If some "blood" is shed, people will see what level of commitment is involved. Leaders make a bold first step when treasured policies or procedures are cut back in order to focus attention on the new path.

Adding a dramatic new policy or procedure also provides boldness to a leader's first moves. Moses reproached the great Pharaoh for redress of the people's grievances. That was unusual. Jesus stood without fear before Pilate and rattled him with his strong and confident serenity before his death. Pilate knew he was in the presence of someone new. God revealed his power before the Egyptians with the Ten Plagues and the parting of the Red Sea. Since favor usually rested with the strong and powerful, this was God's way of communicating that with the *chosen people* things would be different. God's ways are different from ours in bold and startling ways.

If done well, bold moves inspire confidence in followers; otherwise, they may look reckless. After all, only the leader has the clearest idea of the new direction. The followers may be racked with indecision, fear, or uncertainty. They have not been to the new place before. How often do we hear, "But, we have never done it like that before!" These people follow based on their estimation of the leader's competence, confidence, and courage of the leader. So you better communicate all those qualities as fast as possible with strong, visible, and bold first steps. They reveal very quickly just what kind of person is in charge.

Understanding Why People Follow Leaders

There are several reasons that leaders have followers. The reasons fall into two groups: (1) force and fear and (2) rewards. Unfortunately, leaders can simply overpower others. Coercion, force, and power are ancient ways of getting power and, of course, are still popular today. Leaders can also instill fear. Frightened people are weak and tyrants can use that fear to their advantage. However, there are disadvantages to using force and fear. Leaders can never let up or relax. People will follow them only as long as force and fear are applied. People will work only as long as they are watched, and even then, they won't work very well. Therefore, the force and fear must be constantly reinforced. If the leaders ever relax, or worse, turn their backs, they may be attacked. Forceful leaders therefore must always be vigilant, alert, and suspicious of everyone. There is no downtime for these dictators. Their position is always vulnerable to the next claimant to the throne.

The second group involves rewards, or supplying followers with some perceived good. Followers must believe they will benefit by following a leader. It may be plunder and treasure or high wages, for example, but in some way the people must believe *their lives will be better* by following a leader. However, there are disadvantages here also. The people may follow as long as the goodies hold out. When there is no more money, plunder, or treasure, they may just drift away. Money is always a poor motivator. Although leaders can easily buy their followers' services, it is a bad idea to rely on financial gain. Money is a universal commodity. Anyone can supply it. The people won't care, as long as they get it. Leaders who rely on money must recognize they may have no *personal* loyalty from their followers. The followers are loyal only to the cash.

However, perceiving a reward is still beneficial. After all, the Israelites saw the Promised Land as a good they wanted. But the question is, why did they follow Moses? There must have been others who wanted to get out of Egypt. Why did the people find a leader in Moses? Why did they stay with him even when the apparent goodness of leaving Egypt wore off? After force and fear, money and treasure, what is it that causes people to place leadership status on a particular person?

There is another perceived good or reward that is better than money. People can desire the goodness of the *character* of the leader for themselves. They want to be like their leader in some way, so they will stay close to the person, listening to his words or watching her actions. Better still, they will adopt something of that personality themselves. They admire the character and how he or she does things with skill and competence.

A corollary to this idea is the people's desire to be liked by the leader. They want the leader to acknowledge, reward, and encourage them, and they will work hard to receive it. Personal affirmation from an admired leader can even replace money and material rewards. For example, Napoleon remarked how the simple act of dispensing medallion ribbons could motivate his soldiers to amazing feats. He neglected to acknowledge that he would have to be the one handing out the medals! It was recognition *from him* that counted, more than the medal itself. Real leaders have that special relationship with their followers. These next sections will focus on the character traits of good leaders.

Analyzing the Character Traits of Leaders

Of course, parish leaders have an important part to play in the move to the "promised land." Everyone else will look to them for an example to follow. People simply want to know if the boss is really onboard in a personally committed way with the purpose. Does he or she practice what the plan preaches? Does the boss really care about what happens? How much is he or she willing to "put out" for this project? Those answers are crucial to motivating followers. Several dynamics are especially important for anyone hoping to lead. Every one of these characteristics points to one main idea. Every one reveals the credibility of the one who hopes to lead. Credibility is everything. It is the umbrella under which all aspects of leadership character find shelter. We will start our look at the character of leaders by looking at the power and virtue of credibility.

Be Credible

Credibility means there is a connection between words and behavior. Simply put, we *do what we say we will do.* No one will trust an unreliable person who says one thing and does another. Following through on promises spreads a cushion of trust throughout the group that softens the impact of failure or mistakes. Everyone knows that only some projects will succeed, but everyone expects us to practice what we preach. Following through on promises produces a track record of believability, which helps in difficult times. When a leader must present a really bold vision, people will follow even if they find the vision incredible, because they find the leader credible.

Credibility *creates* followers. People will follow the person they *believe* will satisfy their needs. There are many voices clamoring for attention these days, but people will look for the one most likely to produce results. In fact, today more than ever, people are looking for solid trustworthy leaders and they will even do counter-intuitive things if they trust the leader still has their ultimate best interests at heart. They will march toward the Red Sea, change long-standing habits, even bear great hardship, if they believe in the leader. No other personal task is more important than establishing a good track record of trust and believability.

Good leaders tell the truth. Truthfulness is one of the most important qualities of a human being and is even more crucial for leaders. Information is power, so leaders better give good information. Everyone needs reliable facts on which they can depend. They need to have their questions answered, or at least responded to honestly. Nothing builds trust and credibility more than honesty, and nothing destroys it faster than deliberate obfuscation, exaggeration, or lying. Leaders are only as good as their word. Good leaders respect the dignity and intelligence of their followers by giving them the truth.

Credibility comes also to leaders who share the load. If they share in the same work and are willing to share the same burdens, then their followers will feel a kinship with them that breeds loyalty. After all, the leaders are in the same foxhole with everyone else. Everyone develops a strong loyalty toward one another. That loyalty comes in handy at those difficult times when the vision is unclear and the task is uncertain. Followers are more likely to remain loyal to a leader in the uncertain times if he or she has first shown that solidarity with them.

Leaders can model the behavior they want to see in their followers by doing the same work. After all, Moses was asking people to do something they had never even thought of before. How were they supposed to act in the desert? How were they supposed to understand this God who had "chosen" them and not the Egyptians? Moses showed them and, in so doing, gave dignity to their journey. When leaders are willing to perform the tasks of even the lowliest person, they give dignity to every person's participation. No job was unimportant to the Lord. Every person was valued and necessary.

That leadership cemented a loose collection of families scattered across the desert floor into a united people ready to be a "light to the nations."

Credibility comes to those who tell the truth, share the burden, and practice2 what they preach.

Be Bold

This section continues these ideas but on a more personal basis. Good leaders take risks. Good leadership means personal risk. When leaders put themselves at personal risk, when they take a chance, when they put themselves on-the-line for this vision, then people are genuinely moved. They more readily will do as their leaders have done. After all, they have a bold and inspiring example. When leaders guide from the rear, from safety, from a protected place, it diminishes credibility. Why should workers bear the risk alone? Bold leaders go out in front, and those behind will catch that same boldness quickly. Remember, Moses himself, not a committee, dared approach the great Pharaoh.

Leaders show considerable risk especially when they ask for *second-level changes*. When they announce a vision that is out of the ordinary, like Moses moving boldly toward an impassable water barrier, they break open deeper perceptions. After all, blocked by the water and the army, the Israelites thought they would be slaves forever. The Egyptian army and the Red Sea were massive problems for a people trying to escape. Can former slaves win battles or walk on water? No Israelite even thought of it—which is why these are second-level changes. Breaking through that barrier greatly increased Moses' power as a leader and the people's confidence in the Lord.

Leaders can show risk in more personal ways that are even more compelling than physical danger. When leaders become personally vulnerable or transparent to the people, their credibility grows immensely. After all, there is no point in pretending to be perfect or to have never made a mistake. People know that is unreal. Moral strength and personal integrity are, in spite of weakness and failures, much more compelling than untested valor. Everyone knows instinctively that life is hard and that no one emerges unscathed. When a leader acknowledges those mistakes, wounds, or problems freely and without embarrassment, people feel they are dealing with someone who lives in the truth and so more likely will always speak the truth to them. People feel a kindred spirit with a leader who also has wounds. They will learn much from a leader who has learned from life's battles. Moving toward a great and noble goal *in spite of wounds* is the mark of a true leader and a great nation.

Be Skilled

Leaders should be skilled. People admire skill and accomplishment. If leaders are good at the skills they are asking everyone else to do, it is inspirational. While it is not crucial that leaders be the *most* skilled among their followers, it certainly speeds the connection with the crew. Workers will want to be like their leaders in the same proficiency. After all, people want to excel and look to one who is especially competent as a guide. That imitation is the key component of this dynamic. Followers simply want to be like their admired leader. That is probably the most primordial prerequisite for leadership in history, and it still works today.

Moses was careful to show competence in the *right* area. After all, the needed skills must be appropriate. If you go to a doctor to set your broken leg, you don't want to hear about the doctor's spectacular golf game last week. You want the doctor to get about the business of doctoring. Moses was in the prophecy business. He was a spokesperson for the purpose, picture, and plan *of God*, and he was very good at it, despite his fears and despite his weaknesses. We want to make sure we know our real business. We need to make certain we are focused on the *right* goals. After all, the Exodus was not about making better bricks, but about becoming the people of God and living in freedom. Leaders must take a lot of time when assessing a proper purpose *that it is appropriate*. They must develop skills in precisely that area and not become bogged down in peripheral issues.

Be Steady

Good leaders can keep a level head, even when others are losing theirs. Every plan, no matter how well prepared, will encounter unexpected problems. A good leader shows a certain steadiness under fire that stabilizes the inevitable anxiety that problems bring. After all, anyone can be a captain in a calm sea. True mettle is shown in the storm. Remember the Gospel story of the storm on the lake. Peter found Jesus *among the waves* while the others remained hidden in the illusion of safety in the boat (Mt 14:29). Moses faced more problems *after* he left Egypt than before, yet he kept his attention focused on the divinely set goal of the Promised Land. He let neither the Red Sea, nor the grumbling of the people for food and water, nor the Golden Calf distract him or anyone else from the mission. He knew what he wanted and stayed on course.

Remember also that Jesus was deeply centered on the will of his Father in heaven. On some days he would enter a town and, after preaching for a while, would be hailed as a king and a Messiah by a jubilant, grateful audience. On other days in different towns, he would barely escape stoning from a wildly hostile mob. One day a hero; the next, a villain. Throughout it all, Jesus was always himself. His head did not swell with praise nor did he sink into depression with the occasional failure. He was always true to his *core value*. He was always true to his Father's agenda. He never changed the message. Although he would sometimes adapt the teaching style to his listeners, one day telling parables to farmers and the next explaining complicated Scriptures to Pharisees, the basic message always remained the same. That fidelity to his core value allowed for flexibility in method while remaining constant in substance. Nothing could distract him from doing the will of his Father in heaven. Nothing could stop the passion he felt for us. He was steady.

Be Passionate

Good leaders are on fire with zeal to complete the mission. That fire in the soul will spread to everyone around them as well. That passion is important because it will sustain leaders in the difficult times, especially when the goal seems far away or a crisis develops. More important, passion makes the whole project enjoyable. When we feel that strongly about something, we feel even more alive, more vital, and more meaningful. Passion brings the whole self together, focusing energy tightly on one important goal. Passion gives force to the words we use to propel the mission forward, driving the message deep into the hearts of our listeners. People will be impressed at least by the commitment these feelings reveal. Half-hearted speeches and faltering feelings have no power to motivate. If our words are shallow, or weak, or uncertain, our followers will wander away. Leaders must check the level of feelings they have about their goals. Do they create emotion? Do they fire their own imagination?

Passion must still be at the service of reason. It is the head that makes decisions, not the heart. Emotions and feelings are like fuel that can power the engine of the will. Our rational side makes the plan and sets the direction, but it is zeal and passion that provide the energy to make it happen. If it is the other way around, we will be at the mercy of whim, fantasy, and feelings. They come and go so quickly. No group can zig and zag for very long. No group should be governed by feelings. The head must rule the heart.

Passions ruled by the head make us decisive. Zeal for the goal keeps us on track and lets nothing distract us from the chosen path. If something gets in the way, we can quickly choose another path forward. Decisiveness doesn't mean hastiness, it simply means that no time is being wasted. Decisive people get down to business right away because they want to get moving toward the goal. They don't want to lose momentum. Leaders make decisions all the time and each is an opportunity to refocus the vision in everyone's mind. They must constantly make choices about directions, paths to take, and courses to follow. Although there is almost never a perfect choice among options, our strong feeling for the vision helps us decide correctly and clearly for the best one. The courage to choose comes precisely from feeling so deeply about the goal. Passion gives leaders the courage to choose.

After a while, decisive leaders display a certain confidence. Making effective choices time after time produces a track record of success that builds a sense of surefootedness, even in rocky times. That confidence is one of the greatest gifts a leader can pass on to followers. The sense that we can all face the future with confidence, no matter what may come our way, is an extremely liberating feeling. Confidence frees people from fear, which is the greatest obstacle to any move forward. People can accomplish the most when liberated from fear.

Coupled with freedom from fear is the simple idea of freedom itself. The intensity of our passion can never interfere with the basic freedom of people to refuse our vision. People have a right to make their own way in life, to make decisions in their own best interests, even if blatantly shortsighted or wrong. The rich young man walked away from the Lord even after the most excellent teaching on our faith, and yet Jesus let him go (Mk 10:17). Our Lord was sad but still looked at him with love, for he respected his freedom. God created us to be responsible for the gift of life he gave us. We are responsible for the talents he placed within us (Mt 25:15). We cannot usurp that from another. We cannot force someone to our way of living no matter how intelligent, wise, or brilliant we believe our way is. Followers are only real followers when they follow *willingly*. In Egypt the Israelites were slaves; with Moses they were free.

Be Caring

Good leaders take care of their followers. Not that every wish will be fulfilled, but the sense that the leader has paid attention to the concerns of the people helps nourish loyalty. Often only leaders are in the position to handle certain needs. If they do so, then they fulfill an important part of the plan. That concern communicates worth to the followers. It reveals that they are valued members of the team and worth caring for. For example, Moses immediately went to the Lord for food and water for his people. He immediately went to the Lord whenever needs were expressed. He took care of his people. He acted on their behalf and in a way they knew was for their benefit. Good leaders must do the same. *Put simply, good leaders accomplish the purpose and take care of their people.*

The needs of our people are complex. Of course, it is easy to notice the physical needs first. To ignore simple requirements like a comfortable workplace, a reasonable schedule, and common courtesy is ridiculous. No one can seriously ignore these and hope to lead people anywhere. We can show care on deeper levels as well by inviting their participation, honoring honest efforts to help, listening to concerns, and acknowledging good work. Those actions meet the personal needs that members bring to a group.

Boldness, credibility, steadiness, competence, passion, and *a caring spirit* are some of the characteristics that make a leader. A common factor in each dynamic is its important impact on the group in hard times. Each trait is a sustaining factor that keeps everyone marching to the "promised land," despite all kinds of obstacles. Every mission will encounter problems, unforeseen circumstances, and resistance. Without good leadership, every group will flounder. These qualities keep energy focused and directed to the goals despite the many problems that arise.

Real Leaders Are Real People

This may seem like a strange phrase but it involves the most crucial dimension of leadership. The stress and strain of dealing with people who resist change, promote resistance, and cause problems can wreak havoc on a fragile personality. Real leaders must have a strong, healthy, well-developed sense of themselves or they will flounder in the face of those who do. That means leaders must know themselves well and have a clear awareness of their motives and feelings as they go through the day. Of course, everyone has feelings, thoughts, and attitudes about things, but not everyone has *conscious* awareness of them. What we don't know can hurt us. Worse still, it can hurt everyone around us. Acting one way and feeling another can result in confusing signals and unclear communication. Real leaders must know, accept, and like themselves.

Without this self-awareness, or self-acceptance, or self-esteem, deep-seated, unseen, and unhealthy psychological needs can come to the surface and control decisions. These motives, needs, desires, and compulsions can become the leader's actual agenda without his or her awareness of them. Because these motives are selfish, they will not be about the good of the people and certainly not about the vision. Unknown to everyone, the group will slowly revolve around the selfish needs of one person and frustrate real progress toward the "promised land." Though it might be successful at first, the group is bound to fail. Eventually, people will recognize what is going on and resistance will increase. People will resent being used for one person's private agenda. Clearly, this is a crucial issue because the potential for harm is quite real. A real leader must understand the priority of honest self-awareness, self-acceptance, and self-esteem.

There is a natural progression to these healthy personal dynamics that is important to success. Knowing yourself helps develop a mental steadiness that prevents panic in a crisis. *Self-knowledge* then helps build an honest *self-acceptance* and the confidence to accept the challenges of leadership. We simply know what we can do and what we cannot do. Keeping things in perspective is the beginning of wisdom, the most important virtue of all. That wisdom channels our efforts into those areas in which we are more likely to succeed. Rather than taking on the world in some grandiose feeling of exaggerated pride, wise people know their limitations. They succeed more often, and a string of successful accomplishments and self-acceptance will work together to promote self-esteem. All of these dynamics make up the healthy personality and prevent leaders from burning out or becoming cynical. These are the buffers that protect the ego from incorrectly appraising attacks, failures, and setbacks as personal. In other words, wise leaders know the difference between the work being done and the value they have as people. They become completely *involved* in the work without *attaching* their sense of personal value to the result. It means the leaders are real people.

What does it mean to *become* a person? A person is a collection of unique feelings, ideas, behaviors, and especially needs. A "real" person knows, accepts responsibility for, and continues to grow in all those elements of feelings, thoughts, and behaviors. A real person especially understands her own needs and how to appropriately satisfy them. She knows how to *self-regulate* her thoughts and feelings. She is not at the mercy of her own whims or passions, nor does she rely on others to soothe her ego. She is in charge of herself, especially under stress. A real person has achieved a high level of autonomy and is self-motivated to grow and mature further. That process is certainly not automatic. Although we get older with each passing day, we don't necessarily mature. In fact, meeting personal needs in a healthy way is probably the biggest problem area in human development. For example, food is an obvious physical need, but robbing a grocery store is not the right way to get it. Companionship, support, love, and praise are deeper needs, but forcing people to give us these important needs is immature, and dangerous. Knowing what we need and how to get it in a healthy way is a crucial skill we must have *before* taking on a leadership role in an organization.

How does "personhood" develop? Well, we must start with the designer of persons. We must look at the action of God. Our faith really provides the most profound basis for understanding human development. We believe God creates each person, and therefore each person is unique and necessary, with an important role to play in God's plan for his creation. We possess that uniqueness and importance at each moment of our life, from conception through death. That part is automatic. However, we only grow in understanding our role according to natural developmental stages of maturity. That part is a learned skill. No one has ever arrived at full maturity. It is something in which we continue to improve. Leaders must learn to be mature adults. That means they must learn to understand themselves and others honestly, to express themselves clearly, and to accept responsibility for their behavior. They become especially skillful in the art of responsibility. Since they know how to take care of themselves on their own time, they are *free to be completely there for others* in the organization.

Jesus was a powerful model of this. He was always sad, of course, when his teaching would not find a welcome hearing, but that did not stop his mission or change his love for people in the least. He was glad when people accepted faith, but he did not grow grandiose as a result. He was always and simply true to himself. He knew what he wanted and how to get it. He knew what he was about and to whom to be loyal. That is the steadiness of purpose and constancy of attitude that a real person develops when they know, accept, and like themselves. No leader can lead without these personal qualities.

Real Leaders Serve Others, Not Themselves

One way of understanding the work a person does is to ask, "For whom does this person work?" In most organizations you work for the person above you, the one who pays you: the boss. In a pyramidal power structure, the boss is at the top, middle managers are next, and all the line workers are at the bottom. Everyone ultimately works for the boss. He or she is the one everyone wants to keep happy. Real leaders in business reverse that image. They turn the pyramid upside-down. After all, the line workers have more contact with their customers and the company wants the customers to be happy. The line workers make the "sales" and actually deal with the customer, so the line workers deserve the support of the decision makers. Parish leaders can work in the same way. They see themselves as servants of the rest.

For whom do leaders work? If they control what goes on, who controls them? In a healthy Christian organization, there can be only one idea that is truly in charge. The *true best interests* of the people must be the real guiding principles that direct events. We believe that those best interests are also what God wants as well. Real leaders serve only those interests. They discover them, organize them, and bring them into action. Leaders simply guide the accomplishment of *what God already wants for his people*. Real leaders serve that cause, and no other. Real leaders put their power to control others at the service of the best God-given interests of the people. They become servant-leaders.

It may seem strange at first to couple the idea of control with service, but they only make sense together. Uncoupled, each leads to aberrations. Leaders who like to control others, who like to manipulate, manage, and direct others for personal reasons introduce poison into the system. Conversely, leaders who avoid leading, guiding, or directing the people at all, or who bend to every whim, will take the organization in circles. There is nothing more frustrating for workers than to exert all kinds of effort for no gain. Only a balance of control and service will work for success. That balance can only happen if leaders know the difference between personal and public needs. If they use the organization to address or meet personal psychological problems, only disaster can result. Personalization and narcissism are two examples of personal agendas that destroy effectiveness.

Personalization is the most common disaster in groups in which private and public needs mix. As the name implies, leaders take everything personally. All decisions, actions, and events become some kind of continuing referendum on their value and worth as people. These leaders wear their egos on their sleeves. Objectivity is nonexistent. Decisions and actions are understood only as they relate to the leader's self-esteem needs. Personalization prevents any negative feedback from achieving its useful purpose. People will be afraid to speak truthfully about a problem since it will be taken personally. The truth isn't heard, and the group never gets past the leader's problems.

Narcissistic styles are also common. Narcissistic leaders need constant reassurance, support, and praise. A grandiose image hides their fearful unsure selves. These leaders' constant need for affirmation becomes the real goal and agenda of the group. The purpose of the group is to prop up the fragile sense of confidence in the leaders. When people feel as if they are always an audience to their leaders' performance, they suffer from narcissistic leadership. Unfortunately, the reassurance needs are insatiable. They are like a narcotic. Leaders will engineer all activities to revolve around the maintenance of their fragile egos, and it becomes very tiring for everyone involved.

Real Leaders Have Followers

Just because a person has brilliant ideas, or knows exactly what should be done, or has analyzed the future for the most practical purpose, does not mean anyone else will agree. Many times those who undertake leadership cannot understand why no one is following their brilliant plan. How does cooperation happen? Why do people follow leaders? Why should they accept the goals and purpose of just this person? How does a leader connect with that part of his follower's personality that governs cooperation and assent?

As we have seen throughout this book, the answers are found in a closer understanding of what it means to find a purpose. The purpose cannot be found in isolation from the people we hope to lead. We can successfully turn an unorganized group into focused parishioners by taking these steps. The more steps we achieve the stronger the leader-follower bonds. If the goals derive from the people's deepest needs, and the people believe the leader can actually lead them to fulfillment, they will follow.

Good leaders *create* followers. Followers believe the leader will supply the needs, goods, or services they want. These may or may not be conscious needs. The followers, even if they don't know what they want, still believe the leader will get them something good, so they follow. A good leader "knows his sheep." He knows what to provide his followers.

Finally, healthy leaders know what to do to make sure all these dynamics are working well. Because they want the very best for everyone they lead, they will make sure they are in good physical and mental shape to take on leadership. They will not let their own lack of preparation, or immaturity, get in the way of progress. They quickly know when they need attending to and how to improve their effectiveness. Left unmonitored, healthy leaders know they will atrophy, and that is dangerous. Jesus spent every day in prayer, expressing his oneness with the Father. He monitored his relationship with his Father every day. Leaders must also take the time to reflect, meditate, and pray about doing the Father's will.

Another sign of good mental health is the ability to take criticism without collapse and to accept compliments without arrogance. That also requires wisdom. Leaders must balance the objective truth of the critical comment with the reality of their actions. Keeping things in perspective is the beginning of wisdom. Leaders must, of course, pay attention to the comments of their followers. But, again, good leaders know the difference between serving the best interests of their people and catering to whims and selfish desires.

Real Leaders Lead from the Front

All these qualities like bold risk taking and caring must be visible to the people. There is no such thing as a silent or secret leader. It doesn't help to keep powerful motivating factors under wraps. If no one sees the leader take those risks or sees their competence or notices their shared work, the leader won't be effective at moving people anywhere. Leaders lead by being out in front where all those things are noticed. That is where they can do the most good. Visibility is an important key to motivation.

People need to measure the character of the person telling them what to do, and so they need to see him or her in action. The greatness of the mission alone will not be enough. The logic of the purpose alone will not suffice. We need to see the person behind the mission. We need to see what *difference* the purpose has made in *his or her* life. After all the presentations have been made about the purpose, picture, plan, and participation for the great mission, we still need to see *a living example* of someone who has already bought the whole story and is willing to show it!

The more visible the purpose, the easier it is to stay focused on it. There is a wonderful scene in *The Wizard of Oz* where the four main characters begin to walk on the yellow brick road to the Emerald City, and the destination is visible in the distance. Having a visible goal makes every step meaningful. Walking on a winding country path may be beautiful, but it is difficult to determine how far we've come or have yet to go. Good leaders keep the vision visible before their people. Jesus frequently stopped to remind his followers about "the kingdom of God" and how wonderful life there is. Moses did the same for the Israelites, and so must we.

After a while, just the leader's physical presence can remind everyone of the mission. Just showing up now and then in front of the people can serve as a kind of mental shortcut for them to recall what is that binds them all together. Visible presence reinforces and reassures everyone that the plan still holds and is still on track. Working on the plan from inside an office can never be an excuse for remaining hidden, no matter how important that work seems. Being in front of those we want to move *is* the work of a real leader.

Visibility is so important that for many centuries it was one of the main criteria for even choosing leaders. People would not think of following a person they had never seen before. Being sent a leader from some higher authority was simply out of the question. How could they follow someone of unknown character, skills, and commitment? People looked around their own communities and chose the one who *clearly* and *demonstrably* possessed these necessary skills *already*. They *elected* leaders either by ballot or by natural acclaim. That certainly ensured a larger degree of cooperation and harmony of purposes. The people knew who the person was and what his or her values were. That must happen with us before any mission is undertaken. If the leader comes from the outside, some time must be given for the relationship to grow.

Moses had this same concern in his first conversation with the Lord. He was worried that the people would not know who this God was. "Who should I say you are?" he asked. God recognized the importance of this concept and replied, "I am the God of Abraham, Isaac and Jacob." In other words, God announced that he was the God of their ancestors. He was not someone strange and unknown, but a person of familiar care and concern for them. He was "the One" who had spoken *the truth* before. There was no need to get to know a new God. He had taken care of them before and now he had returned in response to their cries to help them again!

Real Leaders Make Constant Improvements

Leaders inspire the best in others when they value and lead improvement. They simply ask, "Can we do things in a better way?" Not a very strange question, really, but one ignored too often. Constant improvement is a key dynamic, one that colors the whole span of all four key words of motivation. Both leaders and followers must join in this crucial and common task that transcends all others, that is, to commit to *constant* improvement. That means they have an important shared understanding or attitude about their work. Whatever they do together, they understand it is not the last and final word on how it is done. The work can always be done in a better way.

That is no poor reflection on workers, but just an honest recognition of human limitations. That understanding is no attempt at nit-picking either. Good leaders know that no task will be perfect. Constant improvement simply means taking an honest look at events with a view toward changing for the better. Far from being some manic and useless appeal to perfection, it simply means we admit we can still learn more, and that we are *not* superhuman. People who commit to constant improvement reveal a beautiful virtue of humility, which is simply the truth about our life. It reveals we can look at everything another way, a more creative way, a more spiritual way, and a more effective way.

While plans may be flawless, actual practice reveals cracks. Usually the actual lived experience reveals unforeseen dynamics, and having the habit of returning to look at them improves the plan for the next time. The focus is on the future and how it will improve with certain modifications. We look at the events, not to place blame or to find fault, but to learn from mistakes and to change. In the Gospels, Peter despaired for a moment about his weakness (Lk 5:8), but Jesus simply invited him to repent and change. Remember, Jesus used the word *repent* over forty times in the Gospels. He did not dwell on our sins so much as invite us to learn from them, to change for the better, and to follow him more closely in the future. It is not the mistake that measures character in an organization, but what they do afterward to improve. Even Jesus felt more joy over one *repentant* sinner than the many with no need to change at all. The desire for improvement defines the character of a Christian and a leader. The Lord invited constant improvement in the healthiest of ways.

Good leaders reflect on events. At the finish of every event, everyone involved should gather and reflect on the experience to discover what worked well and what didn't. In every area we can question how it could have been done better and how it could have been improved given another chance. After all, we *do* have other chances! Motivated people use them well.

Real leaders want feedback. They sincerely seek out reactions from the crew. After all, they are the ones closest to the work itself. They would be the first to know where there is need for improvement, or what needs to be changed. Seeking feedback must be more than a suggestion box on the wall somewhere. A real leader must truly convey the importance of worker input. People can tell very quickly whether someone is interested in what they have to say by how he or she listens and how much time is given to them. Good leadership, then, has a lot to do with being a good listener and taking time. Leaders can reaffirm their interest by reflecting back what they hear either directly or by newsletters or memos of some sort. People like to know their comments are important. If the crew believes their opinions are valued and wanted, they will be more likely to come onboard with a shared sense of responsibility for the group's success.

Leaders should reflect positively on workers, even if events fail. Much too often, reflections can turn negative and judgmental. Nothing shuts down interest in a project like harsh and ill-considered performance reviews, especially when they are given months later and in a superior tone. However reviews can help a great deal if they are done immediately and positively, and if they focus on the work itself and not on the worker, and focus on the future and not on the past. The point is to be humble in the remarks, and wisely acknowledge the good that has been done, as well as what is still needed. After all, no situation is all bad. Every event accomplishes something. Leaders can model this humble reflection and inspire improvement. This reflection process is more like a discovery period, where overlooked events can now be taken into account for the next time.

Real Leaders Make New Leaders

Now we come to the hidden agenda that is the most crucial for success. *The leader's real job is to make new leaders.* While planning a vision and working and doing all the things to achieve the desired goals, real leaders also take note of who among the staff has the potential for leadership. They watch for precisely those qualities in their staff that are needed for leadership and they help bring them forward. That is the leaders' primary task (some say the main task).

A leader cannot be a funnel. It helps no organization to have all decisions and action funnel through one person at the top. A leader must not be that narrow gate through which everything passes. Why have the whole group limited by the ability, personality, and vision of just one person? But if everyone felt a sense of leadership, even if in just their own area, then the whole group would be propelled forward by its combined talents. The group would find the dynamics of the four words exercised at every level of the parish or diocese, down to even individuals *taking responsibility and leadership over their own work.*

A good leader is never too busy. Bad leaders may work hard, but they don't work smart, and smart working is our goal. After all, the very busy, overworked, and constantly stressed leader may be admired as a martyr, but he is really just incompetent. There is no excuse for one person doing all the work. It helps no organization to have its progress pegged to the skill of one person's ability to schedule events and time. It is not only stupidly inefficient, but in many ways, somewhat immoral. It is no credit to a leader who keeps all the work on one desk and allows no help. Imagine the talent bottlenecked by one person! Actually, it is selfish and narcissistic for any person to take over all the activity of the organization. How grandiose to think only he can do something right. Real leaders don't do work, they give work away!

This is more than simple delegation. This is more than just giving the leader a break by helping with office chores. Making leaders of every person in the group has a more primordial justification and we ignore it at our peril. God gives each of us the gift of our own life and we must use that gift to the very best of our abilities. We cannot let anyone else take over what is our responsibility. By making new leaders we provide the opportunity for our people to exercise the autonomy, responsibility, and initiative that is rightfully theirs. We provide them with the chance to grow in the way God intended.

This idea often meets much resistance, ironically from the overworked leaders themselves. After all, if their workload is lessened they might be seen as superfluous. They might lose the illusion of importance. Therefore they see their fellow workers as threats, not as gifts from the Lord. Deliberately planned overwork is very common among parish leaders as well. After all, it provides many psychic benefits, such as a ready excuse for goals not accomplished, an admired martyrlike role, and the illusion of being needed. These are powerful habits of thinking and not easily changed. Coupled with a narcissistic and grandiose personality, it becomes like steel.

Nothing changes an organization faster than the idea of leaders making leaders, of making each person responsible for the overall success. Nothing stops progress faster than leaders keeping all authority to themselves. *That organization can never go past the ability of its boss.* Of course, if the head person is phenomenally talented, some good will occur. But what if she gets sick, or goes on vacation, or loses interest? Why leave fallow the extraordinary talents that lie just below the surface? There is talent and skill everywhere and they must come forward. No leader has the right to ignore or leave untapped the abilities and learning of her followers.

> No one after lighting a lamp puts it under the bushel basket, but on the lampstand, and gives light to all in the house (Mt 5:15).

Becoming a leader actually propels learning and acquiring skills faster than any classroom experience. Even teachers admit they really begin to learn educational topics when they start teaching them. Becoming responsible for student learning actually fuels the drive to know the topic thoroughly. Teaching and explaining forces them to find words and ideas that express in exact terms what were only vague ideas and concepts. In the same way, workers will come to truly appreciate the vision and plan when they must explain it to someone else. Good leaders try to give each person in the organization a chance to also lead.

Real Leaders Form "Apostles" or "Missionaries"

Ironically, these ideas will bring us full circle to the place where we started, but on a much different basis. If each worker feels a sense of leadership, of ownership, and of responsibility to teach others to understand and follow the mission, then he or she will work much harder *even when completely unmonitored.* After all, the worker *knows* what he has to do, he has been thoroughly *trained,* and he *wants* to do it. While unmonitored and unled parish leaders were the very problem stated at the beginning of this book, ironically they can become the pride of the diocese or parish when good leaders bring forward their sense of ownership of the whole mission. Then they become "apostles" or "missionaries" in the best sense. They work without the *need* for direction, using their own abilities *without needing* guidance. Although they work without constant direction, they direct themselves of their own accord, in the commonly accepted vision and according to the commonly accepted standards.

These workers have *internalized* the purpose, picture, and plan completely. They know their part by heart. They also believe in and accept what is expected of them and the standards needed for success. Since they know the standards so well, they can provide their own feedback on progress. As mentioned before, that self-controlled feedback is extremely powerful and effective in guiding behavior. When we control our own feedback, the dialectic between performance and standards produces the fastest improvement in excellence. Although this kind of feedback doesn't take the place of group evaluation and shared reflection on events, it is still a strong motivator for change.

These ideas are certainly not new. They are at the core of our own experience of growing up in families. After all, the glory of parents is to see their children *able and ready* to go off on their own as autonomous and independent persons. At every moment good parents are preparing their children for the day when they will run their own lives. In a trajectory moving from dependence to autonomy, children learn from their parents responsibility, decisiveness, judgment, and wisdom. Where once parents did everything for their children, the children now know how to exercise their own judgment. That judgment is the *internalized wisdom* of the family. Children can control their own feedback about maturing with that internalized standard. This same relationship can exist between leaders and workers.

Like good parents, good leaders are more like mentors; they know a lot about the business and encourage the best in their followers. Good leaders are also like good coaches. The best precedent lies right in our own faith tradition, for this leadership style is already familiar to Christians. A relationship of *encouragement*, or calling out the very best in us, of *challenging* our abilities, of *believing* in our talent, of *coaching* and *training*, of always wishing the very best for us, resembles the behavior of Jesus with his apostles. He formed a band of apprentices around himself.

Real Leaders Form Apprentices

We can look further back than Jesus for an example of apprentice leadership. Moses succeeded beyond his wildest dreams in rescuing his people, but it was a bigger group than he realized. Of course, as any good leader he wanted to meet their needs, but he quickly became exhausted by the size of the effort. In a compelling section of the Book of Exodus, chapter 18, Moses' father-in-law, Jethro, suggests a simple but effective solution. He was speaking to us as well.

> "Now listen to me. I will give you counsel, and God be with you! You should represent the people before God, and you should bring their cases before God; teach them the statutes and instructions and make known to them the way they are to go and the things they are to do. You should also look for able men among all the people, men who fear God, are trustworthy, and hate dishonest gain; set such men over them as officers over thousands, hundreds, fifties and tens. Let them sit as judges for the people at all times; let them bring every important case to you, bur decide every minor case themselves. So it will be easier for you, and they will bear the burden with you. If you do this, and God so commands you, then you will be able to endure, and all these people will go to their home in peace." So Moses listened to his father-in-law and did all that he had said (18:19–24).

Jethro invited Moses to find a few hundred good people of fine character who were able to lead others and set them as leaders over smaller groups. The thousands were grouped into hundreds, fifties, tens, and so on. They took care of things at their own level. Only the big items got to Moses. There is more to this story than just leading by forming small groups. While it makes sense in theory, this is hard to practice successfully. There are a few steps to take.

The first step is to identify and form apprentices. These persons learn the ways of leadership at the very side of the expert. They see firsthand how things are done. They accompany the boss around the place and observe and absorb all that happens. Even the Gospel description of the Twelve reveals them simply as the people who were "with him." Apprentices, like the Twelve, watch and learn. They also try their hand in small matters to practice the art. In Luke 10, Jesus sent his apprentices on a practice mission and offered immediate feedback on their return.

The second step is to challenge the new leader to collect members. Moses cleverly chose group leaders before setting up the groups. After all, leaders *generate their own followers*. Rather than forming groups first and then finding a leader, it's better to reverse that order. We can measure whether a person actually *is* a good liturgy coordinator or youth minister or bible study leader by their ability to attract and form followers. We can tell every new leader that their first and second jobs are to collect members and then to make new leaders. That cycle can go on forever.

The third step is to teach *every* group member apostleship in some way. The Twelve formed every person they met just as they themselves were formed by Jesus. They turned each person into a fellow disciple or apostle. In fact, an underlying theme of every parish could be the same: to make every person an apostle. If all work is still being done by one or two leaders, even if charismatic, skillful, and competent, the whole group has a bottleneck. They are it! *They are emptying the talents of the rest who remain content to listen and follow.*

For example, if you had worked long and hard on a speech, and then found out a parishioner knew more about the topic, would you be tempted to invite that person forward? That would be a powerful statement. If each parishioner were invited to take upon themselves the responsibility, the work, and the real joy of the parish mission, who could predict how powerful a presence that parish would be in its community? Every parishioner becomes a leader in his or her own area and forms new members. As leaders, they made new leaders and the cycle continues.

The fourth step is to give up the idea of protecting "turf." The most beautiful side effect of leaders making new leaders is reducing envy and jealousy—the killers of organizations. However, since *everyone* in the group is being groomed for leadership there can be little need for one coveting another's position. If one person shows a desire for a more prominent role, a wise leader will encourage such movement. Precisely because leaders are on the lookout for people with initiative, they can hardly be protective of their own turf. Just the opposite occurs. People are encouraged to take over once in a while. After all, good leaders believe in their people.

The fifth step uses ritual celebrations to add an emotional aspect. They provide an emotional cement that solidifies the promises and commitments of leaders and workers. Ritual celebrations work especially well at the beginning and ending periods of significant events. Just as the baptism of Jesus launched his ministry with wonderful sights and sounds, so a celebration can be used to launch a new small group, new minister, or program. They serve to publicly declare the importance and gravity of the moment. Our sacraments already celebrate those meaningful spiritual life events. Banquets, lunches, award ceremonies, public announcements, Masses, paraliturgies, and blessings also celebrate important events in the life of the Church.

Chapter Five

Going to the Wrong Place

We are presenting quite a picture of a leader in these pages. The picture may seem to show some kind of superperson, unrelated to the mortals and flawed individuals we find here on Earth. Certainly the leader we envision is not meant to be superior, far from it. We read in the book of Genesis that God created all of us in his image. The Genesis story goes on to reveal in more detail the qualities of that image, which reveal that our human nature was created in goodness and freedom. They reveal a basic equality among the sexes and among all people. We are to be helpmates to each other (Gen 1:1–2:23). In the Garden of Eden we lived a true human life as God intended. Because of Jesus we remain today good, free, equal, and helpmates to each other.

Leaders cannot violate any of those "Garden of Eden" virtues while exercising their office. If this happens, the group will be well on its way to the wrong place. Wherever that is, it will be a place no one will want to stay. Therefore, leaders must show great care whenever they dare to exercise any kind of control, influence, or management over another. Leadership is a great honor and comes with an awesome responsibility to treat all people with the same respect and love they receive from God. There are two main ways that leadership can deny the basic goodness, equality, freedom, and helpmate-ness of people. They can either lead too autocratically, an act of despotism, or too weakly, an act of abandonment. We will examine those two types in more detail now.

Dealing with Poor Leadership

There are two ways that poor leadership can cause problems among the people: by excessive direct attack or by excessive neglect. In both cases the leaders assault the worth, value, and dignity of their followers' sense of themselves. First, leaders can wound a person by some kind of direct assault, either physically or emotionally. It may be an act ranging from belittling the follower's efforts to severe physical beatings. Second, leaders can attack personal dignity through the act of abandonment. That may be an event anywhere from ignoring a person to actually physically abandoning them at important times when the leader *should* be present. In that case the person is perceived as not worthy of care and attention. In each case, the person may either retreat from the leader in fear or lash out in anger, even if covertly.

Not everyone is harmed by traumatizing leaders. People who have stable, mature, and secure personalities will not appreciate such leaders and may seek another place to work, but will not necessarily be harmed. They have learned not to "take things personally." They know how to take the leaders' actions in context and put them into perspective. However, these people are rare, and their presence is no excuse for leaders to act irresponsibly. Chances are a traumatizing leader will affect many people. They will tend to react in fear or in anger.

These feelings tend to predominate in traumatized individuals. As a result, they might begin to develop primitive emotional strategies for response, much as a child would. These ideas are important to address because the consequences of inaction are important. But first, it might be a good idea to indicate some of the psychological traditions from which these ideas derive.

While there is not total agreement among different personality theories, in general the healthy "self" is the name given to that center of the personality that organizes the thoughts, feelings, and actions that combine to make up a person's unique personality. In that "center" a person develops and stores the inner images or representations of the world. They are the "templates" of people and events that a person crafts over the years. They are the habitual ways of understanding life. Psychoanalytic psychologists call them "transferences," cognitive psychologists call them "schemas," system psychologists call them "roles," psychodynamic theorists call them "internal objects," and behaviorists call them "learned responses." They are the stories we use to explain the world around us. After a few years they become deeply ingrained in the psyche and color the perspective of the world. They become our "Weltanshaunng" or world view.

In the first few months of life, a person begins to form basic images of the world according to primitive ideas of pleasure, pain, good and bad. The world has too much information for such a little mind to encompass, so the child tends to collect all experiences into these few simple categories. The child puts people, events, and experiences into categories based on primitive emotional states of pleasure, pain, good, or bad. Of course, the categories will become more complex as time goes on, but later experiences of people or events will be strongly guided by these early ones. What determines their strength? The *intensity, frequency,* and *duration* of the emotional state or experience determines the depth, power, and durability of the image or inner representation. Similar experiences over many years form the deepest and longest-lasting impressions. While we believe that no personality is set in concrete, and that change is *always* possible, the longer the habits are in place the more durable they become.

The "self" is a constant and stable subjective experience of that sense of "me-ness" we experience every day. The self perceives the world, integrates the data, and finally, acts to achieve a purpose. The self is the sum total of all those inner representations, their associated feelings, and the capacity to act in the world guided by those images. The building blocks of the self are threefold: the genetic and environmental endowment, the impact of the primary caregivers (e.g., the parents), and the choices the person makes about both. If the genetic endowment is good, the caregivers are affirming, and the choices are wise, then the self emerges as "real-self" (i.e., self-activating, spontaneous, integrated, and conscious of motives, feelings, and thoughts). Most important, the real-self is able to act in the world responsibly.

The real-self is able to give back to the word all that it has taken in. The real-self has an overall sense of worth, dignity, honor, and value. That self-praise plus the ability to act effectively combine to make self-esteem. Praise plus accomplishment combine to ensure a strong self-esteem. Praise without accomplishment is mere flattery, while accomplishment without praise leads to resentment. Together they keep the self healthy and intact. The basic sense that the self is valuable is the essential ingredient that must be inviolable. Severe trauma attacks this self-worth, denying the value of the self.

These dynamics describe the self in psychological terms and are certainly useful in the *assessment* of personnel situations, but they are not as easy to use in *treating* or actually *changing* problem behavior. Psychological theories can be an elegant but very intricate way of understanding personnel problems and the complex motives people might have under stress. But the concepts are more useful in regular therapeutic settings than in actual interventions at work or in the parish that help change behavior. Since we are in parishes and not counseling rooms, we need to find a system that works on-site, and without the involvement of complicated psychological dynamics.

Systems theory and family therapy are two related psychological schools of thought that developed in the last forty years as a more effective way of actually fostering real and lasting change in people. They do not dwell as much on the past or on the reasons people are the way they are, but more on how they can move ahead in a healthy way. These schools especially recognize the power of fellow parishioners with the problem person. These theories are useful here precisely because they deal with people as part of larger groups. Any group forms a "system" of social interactions that powerfully influence behavior. A well-ordered group enhances the mental health of anyone in it and guides behavior according to well-understood rules. These are the ideas that produce change. Most specially, they are nonpathologically oriented; that is, they focus on the strengths already present instead of the weaknesses. They are much more useful in actually making a change in relationships because they use talents, skills, and abilities already present in the person rather than trying to build what is not there.

For example, we believe that every person has a natural desire to excel, to belong to a group of like-minded people, and to have his or her work affirmed by others. The best system for change will capitalize on those deep-seated needs. Their main themes are incorporated in the four key words of purpose, picture, plan, and participation, which combine to satisfy each of those needs. Systems and family theory interventions focus on behaviors that accomplish and fulfill those needs rather than on more complex understandings of inner mental states. Together, both systems help. One tells us much about what is going on inside a person, while the other helps guide actual change for the better.

The types of interventions our Lord used in the Gospels ironically revealed many of the same techniques as a systems and family theory approach, as well as an understanding of the deeper turmoil of the inner object relations inside people. He called himself "the good doctor" (Lk 5:31) who is interested in people getting better, not condemning them for being sick. Jesus rarely gave anyone a hard time for the mistakes they made in life, but focused more on repentance—the changes we make for future and new behavior. He often prescribed behavior as a means of fostering behavioral change, rather than waiting for insight to happen. For example, he told the woman caught in adultery, "Go, and sin no more." He told the apostles, "Follow me." These commands summarize his whole approach. Not that insight is unimportant, but the lesson is clear: Imitate behavior and insights will follow. Moses changed the behavior of the Israelites when they sinned at Mount Sinai by worshipping the Golden Calf. Supported by the strong actions of the whole tribe of Levi, Moses called them back to their original behavior. Simply put, good healthy behavior, supported by the whole group, will powerfully influence the individual behavior of any one person in the group. Rather than force a change, it will inspire it. Healthy group behavior has that natural consequence.

The behavior of traumatizing leaders has its own natural and inevitable consequences, which fall heavily on those being led. These followers can show behavior that actually mirrors their leaders' excessive style. For example, followers will exhibit either excessively withdrawn (fear) or overly aggressive (angry) responses when subjected to a traumatizing leader. However, their behavior can also become more sophisticated, subtle, clever, and ingenious. The self of the especially wounded person has been severely attacked. She therefore might choose a strategy for protection that hides the self for safekeeping behind a set of behaviors that mask it and puts forward a "false-self" before the world. That false-self uses every resource available in amazingly clever ways to achieve the purpose of defending the real-self. It is not necessarily a malicious goal for it arises out of pain, the pain of a wounded sense of worth and dignity. It arises from the irrational fear of worthlessness. The behaviors of these followers are more rooted in fear and pain than in evil intent.

The purpose of the false-self is to keep the world "at bay" and away from the fragile real-self buried deep in the unconscious. This false-self quickly learns to "read" the environment and people for signs of danger, which it always expects and anticipates. It might quickly adapt to changing circumstances to literally "be" whatever it needs to be to be safe. For example, the false-self may "cling" to a strong person and become a lifelong protégé to a succession of powerful people. That behavior helps it hide in the shadow of another. It may be aggressive one moment and ingratiating the next. It may be wonderfully obedient and saintly one time and wildly enraged the next. The false-self trusts few people, and learns a variety of clever, subtle, and sophisticated strategies to hide the real-self inside and away from the perceived dangerous world.

Because these behaviors arose from a sense of being attacked, and involve strategies for the person's very sense of survival, and because these strategies developed very early in life with primitive and intense emotions, they are strong, deep seated, often subconscious, and, most importantly, used. After all, the person must win; her subjective sense of survival is at stake.

For example, if the direct assault is particularly massive and severe, the person learns it may be useless to fight back directly. He therefore automatically, and maybe even unconsciously, develops a strategy of passive-aggression. He might retreat into a outwardly passive stance, but fight back indirectly, secretly, and unobtrusively. For example, while outwardly obeying the rules, the person may be spreading false rumors about the leaders. Conversely, the false-self may be aggressive-passive. Here, he might act out of direct revenge and rage, and then retreat into his "victim" status as a misunderstood unfortunate in the organization and play on the guilt of others to elicit compassion. Some people may also unjustly use their minority status as an excuse to blame others and manipulate compassion by a clever false-self system. Of course, minorities have been and continue to be unjustly victimized in the workplace. But sometimes it is difficult to separate the good from the bad use of that status to achieve justice. A leader's attack may arise from prejudice or from the objectively poor quality of the person's work.

Fear and rage are powerful motivators and energizers of action. The false-self is highly motivated to become an expert at reading the personalities of the organization for weakness and vulnerability, which it will exploit for survival's stake. Ironically, the false-self, formed as a defense against suffering, can be extraordinarily callous to the sufferings of others. After all, if you believe you are falling over a cliff, you will not mind the damage you do to a friend's clothes as you desperately cling to them to keep yourself from falling to your death.

There is an old football phrase that says, "The best defense is a good offense." The false-self uses this idea well. Rather than wait for the next inevitable attack, the false-self will seek to manipulate the environment to its own needs. That way it is in control and feels safe. Overcontrolling behavior and the need to manipulate others reveal a desperate fear of spontaneity. When the moment is unknown, the false-self is reminded of the terror of the unexpected attacks of childhood and fights back with controlling strategies.

This is not a hopeless scenario. The four key methodologies of purpose, picture, plan, and participation are built on a firm bedrock of hope, and informed by the disciplines of psychology and sociology as well as the beliefs of our faith. Knowledge of false-self strategies simply informs leaders about certain behaviors. It also motivates them to feel more compassion for the traumas endured by their followers and to find truly effective and genuine means of healing. Knowledge of the power of purpose, picture, plan, and participation provides the tools to guide healthier behavior and a cushion to soften the impact of problem people.

The four key ideas of purpose, picture, plan, and participation combine to produce healthy results because they direct all activity in a parish. Each one sets a direction for leadership behavior and even for personal growth. Together, they corral problem behavior behind clear boundaries. The consequences of a successful purpose, picture, plan, and participation system are immediate and healthy. The consequences of failure are enormous. Without that direction or some reasonable equivalent, many will flounder. When parish leaders don't know what they are supposed to do around the parish and with the people they lead, they end up doing nothing (and trying to get away with it). Work levels drop, they do less and less, and it all seems strangely okay. After all, no one notices, no one cares, and no one pays any attention. What else can people conclude than it must be acceptable to those in charge. In fact, that lazy behavior becomes reinforced by the leader's acquiescence. It also becomes deeply entrenched.

Left to themselves for too long, unmonitored and unnoticed parish leaders and parishioners will set their own behavior standards, as low or as eccentric as they might be, and these standards become exceedingly difficult to change at a later date.

Precisely because people want and need direction in life, they will fill in the vacuum left by directionless leaders and set their own idiosyncratic standards for ministry. If no one above feels the need for standards, then the natural human discomfort of role ambiguity will impel people to find *some* kind of role that is individually and idiosyncratically determined. Precisely because they are self-set standards, they become quite strong and very difficult to change, after even a short while. Ironically, because people like to excel they will tend to set their own standards low. Each leader settles into "his or her own thing" and, ironically, feels as if he or she is doing a good job! After all, who can comment on standards only one person knows? Ministers become "independent contractors," no longer effectively part of any larger group like a diocese or parish but a law unto themselves. These parishioners are notoriously difficult to bring on-board any common project. Of course, there are always exceptions, but this dynamic describes an all-too-familiar pattern.

The principle is simple. When there is a lack of leadership, information, or standards for doing things from the top, people simply fill in the blanks with their own ideas. For example, when there is little information about a new project or program, they will gladly supply rumors and innuendo according to their own bias or preferred viewpoint. When there are no standards for doing a job, they will supply their own and at their own level. At first, there might only be confusion and wonder, but then a range of more maladaptive defenses can take over. People can feel anger, rage, disappointment, and even fear. Most of this can also be unconscious or at least unarticulated, but it nevertheless guides behavior that is destructive.

Younger parish leaders are particularly susceptible to this dynamic. They are the first to feel a little overwhelmed by new parish experiences, and rightly look to pastors or bishops or other senior parish leaders for some guidance or example to follow. They appropriately wonder what the right thing to do is. They may also interpret inaction as a lack of caring, or worse, a statement about their worth as persons. If there is an absence of any *clear and authoritative* direction, they can react with a sense of anger or surprise at being left in the lurch and then quickly work out behavior standards for themselves. Later, those standards are hard to change by the leaders who ignored them in the first place. Ironically, once personal standards are set, the support longed for at the beginning is rejected later on. Leaders are then rejected as interfering with personal style. While this "abandonment" notion receives a lot of attention in serious psychological difficulties, it also can appear on much smaller scales, such as the day-to-day relationship between leaders and people.

These personal and idiosyncratic standards will vary greatly from leader to leader and can cause great confusion among parishioners, who go through the same dynamics when confronted with the inactivity, confusion, or absence of their parish leaders. There is a multiplier effect in these cases. Any difficulties will be magnified precisely because leaders are in such central positions surrounded by many people,

Independent contractor–type parish leaders often justify their style of ministry with an appeal to the goodness of diversity or a respect for their unique gifts and style. After all, isn't everyone different? However, parishioners see more than stylistic differences; they see a real variance in the content of ministry and even in faith itself from parish to parish. This variance includes the requirements for sacraments, priestly and leadership availability, and even the attitude toward the institutional Church itself. Catholicism can seem radically different depending on which parish you attend. That confuses people.

While well-meaning pastors may try to instill some coherent direction within their parishes, it has little credibility when parishioners have such easy access to what is happening elsewhere. For example, one parish may have a well-developed baptismal educational program for parents consisting of several parent meetings, while next door the pastor will immediately baptize anyone who walks in the door. The credibility *of both* is lessened in the eyes of the people. If direction is not set from above the pastoral level, then pastors and leaders will find their efforts undermined. The only solution is to have a coherent system of leadership present at every level of the diocese, from the bishop, through the chancery, through the parishes, and even in families.

Of course, these reflections are not meant to blame anybody for anything. Many of these behaviors are rooted in intense personal pain and suffering, even if on an unconscious level. People are usually not malicious in their motivations but act according to the world as they perceive it and the primitive emotional strategies developed to deal with it. If the world appears dangerous to them, then behavior is predictable. These ideas simply suggest there are natural consequences for natural psychological dynamics. Rarely are leaders and workers actually malicious, although their behavior may seem so. Usually, they are just not informed. Fortunately, both can always improve with the few simple ideas from the tradition presented here. Good leadership is certainly not paternalistic or condescending, nor does it seek to completely run every aspect of parish ministry. Ironically, it allows the best in people to come forward. It respects the model of leadership already found in our own tradition. It respects the freedom of individuals as well as the legitimate authority of Church leadership. While providing only a few simple directions, the true diversity found among parish leaders can be directed to a common vision each parishioner along with their leaders have helped set and want to achieve. This will not happen automatically, though. The Lord expects us to do our part, and act in a way that takes human nature and the psychology of leadership and motivation into account. The consequences are important.

Convincing People Who Don't Want to Go

Even Moses had grumblers. Not everyone was "onboard" the exodus journey and some even plotted against him. Nothing surprising in that. People usually don't like change. Even if present circumstances are painful, at least they are known and familiar. "The devil we know is better than the one we don't." That summarizes most efforts to stop change. After all, while it may be difficult, who knows if the change will bring something good? What if it gets worse? Then we lose even the little we have now. That is a real fear that leaders should take seriously. These thoughts are important indicators of powerful psychological barriers that need changing. If we don't respect the difficulty of change, we might drag these problems with us into the new situation and not even realize it.

On a deeper level, people wonder if they'll have what it takes in the "new land." Facing any challenge immediately reminds us of our inventory of resources to meet it. We might discover feelings of inadequacy or uncertainty about internal strength, and a general unease about our ability to do the new things. No one wants to look incompetent, so uncertain parishioners feel they must do something to stop the change. They resist.

We might find a host of petty details suddenly flooding the work process, all to distract the focus on change. Amendments, suggestions, and alternatives will come pouring in from fearful parishioners to clog the wheels of progress and derail the new program. While paying lip service to the new goals, some people secretly, and maybe even unconsciously, lay down clever blocks and obstacles to the new direction. They might seem to be joining the team and embracing change, but later we find our efforts subtly undermined, sabotaged, and resisted at every turn. Rumors, false information, and innuendo are the favorite ammunition of these passive-aggressive types. These workers are terribly destructive and frustrate real progress. They're like land mines. Secreted in the organization, they go off when we least expect. It's better to understand and address their issues than ignore them. They will not disappear with our inaction.

Change represents loss before it reveals gain. People lose their old way of doing things, familiar habits, and ways of thinking. Certain people might lose prestige, their status, or a favored way of operating. As mentioned earlier, some might resent realignment with a leader who was absent when really needed before.

Many simply fear the unknown and hold on with a white-knuckle grip to what they have now. Most important of all, the change may be a threat to *authentic core values* of the person or organization. Every group has these core values or basic self-understandings and they must be safeguarded throughout the change process. We cannot stress enough how important it is for leaders to understand these change and resistance dynamics because they will greatly influence the chances of success.

Every change involves some kind of loss. For people used to routine and the familiarity of regular ways of doing things, that is difficult. Loss is one of the most powerful and important of human events, and it happens all too frequently. In truth, very little stays the same in our world. People die, grow old, or move away. Companies evolve, the economy declines, kids grow up, and, of all things, even the weather changes. Despite the regularity of change, people still go to extraordinary lengths to avoid dealing with loss.

Yet every loss means something new is arriving. For every "good-bye," there is a "hello" to something new. Along with the fear of losing we also possess the excitement of getting. If the new direction is *faithful* enough to core values, *noble* enough to inflame our passions, and *needed* enough to inspire action, then that goal will pull us into a new future. We will want to "get it." If the new "promised land" is vividly portrayed using each of the four elements of leadership, the past will no longer appear better. A clear purpose begins that rationale for change. Then, a vivid picture excites the imagination and helps break down resistance further. The picture we paint is the gain we move toward. An emotional picture adds power to breaking resistance and moving us forward. Next, a carefully designed plan reassures everyone that someone is in charge and that our ship is not drifting. Finally, our participation co-opts resistance.

Resistance is strongest when change comes as a surprise, or when it is someone else's idea. Moving people against their will almost never works. A simple physical demonstration reveals this. For example, if you stand with your hand on another's shoulder and gently push, the other person will instinctively resist that threat to equilibrium and push back. However, if you are dancing together, then those pushes are expected and, in fact, invited. A wonderful dance follows. No matter how good the message is, no matter how necessary we feel the change is, no movement will occur unless it corresponds to the will of the people. All these decades of psychotherapy since Sigmund Freud still reaffirm this powerful but often forgotten idea. We cannot really change another at will. With skillful leadership, we can guide the changes people *already* want to make. Leaders must include their followers in the whole process.

When we are part of the purpose or mission formation, when we help in picture painting, and when we add to the planning process, then we are completely *inside* the project. Our own ego is connected to the project's success. We become co-responsible for accomplishing the mission. We have internalized the mission. We are finally onboard. After all, we want the boat to sail, because we're in it! We want the goal achieved because it has become our goal. Good leaders take the time to carefully craft a rational, emotional, planned, and participatory image, for in our foggy and misty future it is the beacon of hope.

Helping the Problem Follower

Moses encountered the event that sooner or later befalls every leader—the problem follower. For Moses, it was Aaron. The people came to Aaron and complained about the long delay in Moses' return from Mount Sinai. In his absence, the attention of the people wandered. Once again, if the leader is not visible, present, and available, wandering attention is the inevitable result.

> Moses saw that the people were running wild (for Aaron had let them run wild...)(Ex 32:25).

We don't know why it happened. Perhaps the Israelites felt abandoned, perhaps they lost faith in Moses' return as the text reads, or perhaps they thought they had a better plan than the Lord's. Maybe Aaron also felt these emotions and silently wished for Moses' failure. Human frailty abounds in this story. People sometimes succumb to more motives in moments of weakness. That has certainly happened a few times in the Scriptures, and in parishes today. It will happen in any group of people as well when an opportunity for easy power comes along. In our story, the Israelites asked for a new god, a new leader. Aaron quickly acquiesced. He built the Golden Calf and led the people in idolatry. Perhaps worried by the absence of Moses, Aaron led the sacrifices that brought unity to the people who were alone and afraid in the desert. How quickly they rewrote history as well. The people declared that it was this new god who had brought them out of slavery! History is a malleable phenomenon. It is remembered not so much as facts, but as *useful* facts filtered through the prism of present needs. The past serves present purposes. People readily see it differently depending on their needs now.

> And they said, "These are your gods, O Israel, who brought you up out of the land of Egypt!" (Ex 32:4).

A closer look at the Israelites' behavior reveals perhaps a more selfish motivation. The God of Moses required discipline, character, and courage—ennobling, yes, but difficult. Perhaps the people were looking for a little revelry. The story also reveals the relationship between anger and reason in dealing with problems. As usual in biblical accounts, God is presented as the angry one, appeased only by the cleverness, bargaining, or pleading of some prophet. Here Moses interceded and reminded the Lord of his own grand purpose.

> "Remember Abraham, Isaac, and Israel, your servants, how you swore to them by your own self, saying to them, 'I will multiply your descendants like the stars of heaven, and all this land that I have promised I will give to your descendants, and they shall inherit it forever.' " And the LORD changed his mind about the disaster that he planned to bring on his people (Ex 32:13–14).

Keeping the focus on the goal acts as a kind of containment device that corrals the emotions. Uncontrolled anger is dangerous. When the heart rules the encounter, people say and do things they regret later. Uncontrolled rage obscures the real issues. If the battle becomes personal, if it becomes a referendum based on ego, no progress will be made. Discussion can easily degenerate into name-calling and insults. The issue then changes to defense against personal attack. All respect for the person disappears and decisions arise from vindictiveness. For a good leader, there is *no* excuse for disrespect.

The four key words of purpose, picture, plan, and participation provide the clear beacon in the darkness to which we can return. Yet, even Moses couldn't contain himself and destroys the tablets in a rage. Ironically, Aaron calms him with almost the same words Moses had used with the Lord. The guiding principle behind all actions with a problem follower is to return to the purpose, picture, plan, and participation dynamics. The breakdown occurred somewhere in the execution of those words, so there must be a return. However, problems do not occur in an emotional vacuum. There is almost always an emotional issue that must be addressed as well.

The first principle in dealing with the problem follower is an understanding of the emotions, rage, and anger that might possibly arise *both* within the leader and the follower. It is very hard not to take resistance personally. The excitement the leader generates for the mission comes from his or her own feelings. When these feelings are belittled by a person attacking the mission, it hurts. The leader resents the person's resistance, but the person also resents the leader's resistance. The parishioner may feel things were just fine until this new mission came along. If these emotional dynamics are left unattended for too long, no one will remember the original issue. It becomes a must-win situation for each of the participants since the dignity of their very sense of self is at stake.

The leader must intervene to effect a solution. There can be no abdication of that responsibility, or pretty soon every one will go off in different directions. By addressing the emotional side first, the leader prevents clouding of the issue. That does not mean the emotions disappear; that takes time. But they will lessen in intensity, hopefully enough for some reasonable discourse to ensue. Understanding the dynamics of change, feeling empathy with workers' concerns, and showing interest in the real welfare of the person help detoxify emotional encounters. A leader who can feel the workers' experience and "see" it through their eyes will react sensibly and with compassion, not with anger.

Once the situation has become more rational, the leader can solve the problem with four steps. He or she must (1) know the truth, (2) tell the truth, (3) show the truth, and finally, (4) recommend or invite a solution from the person for the problem. Let us look at each item in this list.

1. Know the Truth

The leader must know the truth of the situation. Every bit of pertinent information must be collected. Moses mistakenly acted too fast, and asked questions later. As a result, the tablets were broken and people were killed. Acting too quickly is acting badly. Nothing destroys credibility faster than acting on information that later turns out to be false. Reputations might be destroyed for no reason and that can only sow seeds of revenge and resentment. A leader must know the truth, and that takes time. Therefore she must listen, investigate, question, and ponder before acting. The need to act quickly should not overrun the importance of the careful collection of facts.

How does a leader organize all the facts that pour in? The easiest way to understand the problem is in the context of purpose, picture, plan, and participation. The leader can look at most problems as some kind of difficulty in one or more of those areas. For example, does the parishioner have a problem with his participation? Does he have unclear standards and expectations? Does he disagree with the standards? Does he need more affirmation or attention? Does he need a better picture, or more motivation? Does he disagree with the purpose? Is there a problem with the plan, training, or goals set? Looking at all the information in the light of these four key words brings some order to what might be a chaotic jumble of facts and events. These words connect them all into a coherent picture that helps both the leader and the worker understand what is going on. They also help suggest solutions.

2. Tell the Truth

The problem follower must be told that his behavior has been noticed and found wanting. The leader must also say what element of the four *p* words is the problem. If there is to be any kind of sanction, the person must know what behavior it is directed toward. The motive, after all, is *improvement*, not *punishment*, so the person must know which behavior is in question and why. How else will she know what needs to improve? Telling the truth must be as clear and direct as possible. We do our follower no favors by sugar-coating or shading the truth. Excessive diplomacy can really become excessive confusion. Leaders need to be direct. However, that does not mean bluntness or crudeness. It does mean keeping language respectful, polite, and professional. It also means not taking thirty minutes to say what could be said in five.

> Moses saw that the people were running wild (for Aaron had let them run wild, to the derision of their enemies) (Ex 32:25).

Implicit in this description is the importance of action. Aaron's lack of attention to a growing problem led to chaos. Doing nothing becomes its own problem added to the one we are trying to solve. A leader who allows a problem to continue only invites more problems. People will simply assume that the problem behavior is tolerated and maybe even approved. Worse still, they will lose faith in the original purpose. Inattention creates a leadership vacuum, which brings forth challengers and rivals. They exploit the opportunity created by an absent leader. The problem follower may be testing the mettle of the leader, gauging depth of commitment, or challenging the purpose. Any of these deserves immediate action. The leader cannot remain passive. Quickness does not mean precipitousness, however. Moses acted too quickly. It simply means the machinery for solution is set in motion. In general, a quick response is better than a late one, as long as sufficient information is available on the truth of the situation.

3. Show the Truth

The leader must also show some visible and objective corroboration of the facts. The more the better. This keeps the whole process objective and ensures against prejudice or bias. Objective verification may include pictures, witness testimony, or other irrefutable evidence. This may also be the time for including more people in the intervention. At first, the meeting should be kept as private as possible. In general, give public praise and private pans. No need to add public humiliation to the situation. That only fuels the fire of revenge and closes off dialogue. It is generally better to pull the person off to the side away from the crowd for a private meeting first.

> "If another member of the church sins against you, go and point out the fault when the two of you are alone. If the member listens to you, you have regained that one. But if you are not listened to, take one or two others along with you, so that every word may be confirmed by the evidence of two or three witnesses. If the member refuses to listen to them, tell it to the church; and if the offender refuses to listen even to the church, let such a one be to you as a Gentile and a tax collector (Mt 18:15–17).

If no progress is made, or if the person refutes the information, then it may be necessary to show the truth in the manner described above. Of course, the follower is also given a chance to explain, if possible, alternative explanations for the evidence. It may also be possible for the follower to posses information not available to the leader. This is the time to ask for it and evaluate together its appropriateness. This is an important point. The person may have truly discovered something wrong. Wise leaders respect (love?) their enemies. They just might reveal some truth that has been closed for too long.

4. Recommend or Invite a Solution to the Problem

The leader must not just "dump" on the person and walk away leaving a devastated follower. Such a person will only seek revenge or simmer in resentment. This final step reveals the main intention of the action. This is the most important step of all because it reaffirms the basic *relationship* of the person to the group and the mission. We want the person to feel wanted and affirmed. Recommending a solution also affirms that the four *p* words remain the focus of all activity, and that the desire is to return to it as quickly as possible. Our purpose in recommending a solution is *improvement* of the person, not punishment.

Jesus used the word *repent* over thirty times in the Gospels. It is a wonderful word that means "change." For Jesus, it meant change for the better. Jesus forgives so we might learn from our mistakes, grow deeper in faith, and develop stronger character. We will live more joyful, meaningful, and happier lives. No wonder God is so eager to forgive. He wants us to have that kind of happy life. He wants us to move from behaviors that block it to behaviors that bring it to us. He is on our side! How wonderful to know we can change! We can repent. *That we sin says nothing about our character. What we do afterward says everything, and what we do is repent.* That is why we focus on the "sins" of the follower. Our desire is to help the person grow, mature, and develop. We have the same hopes, dreams, and attitude for the person that God has for us.

Inviting a solution from the person himself also improves the chances for compliance. He is more likely to follow through on what he himself recommends. Inviting him also shows respect for his intelligence and returns him to the sense of "team" that we want for everyone in the group. It brings him back "inside" the fold. If nothing comes to mind, the leader can suggest a solution as a point of departure for discussion. The focus remains on a solution and not on the person himself.

What if none of this works and the person is still unrepentant? That happens. The Gospel invites us to let the person go. Sometimes we might have to just separate ourselves from the person who stubbornly refuses to return. He will just have to leave the group, be fired, laid off, or whatever is appropriate to effect separation. Moses drew a clear line in the sand in his case by returning to the original purpose. He boldly asked everyone to recommit themselves to the Lord. It not only reaffirmed his leadership but reminded everyone what the original plan was.

> Then Moses stood in the gate of the camp, and said, "Who is on the LORD's side? Come to me!" (Ex 32:26).

If the problem is extremely severe, it may call for rooting out all contrary forces of the entire organization. The group cannot go in all directions at once. The whole point of the four *p* words is to focus activity toward the accomplishment of *one* mission. Moses felt the need for this drastic action in the episode with the Golden Calf (Ex 32:1–35).

Discovering Where Problem Behaviors Develop

There is a broader way to think about where problems develop than just the four key words. We can funnel the problem areas down to two simple categories. Problem behaviors inside the parish will either be in the parishioner alone or in the leadership style of those in charge. Of course, we also have to admit some combination of the two, but generally, problem behaviors will fall into one of these categories.

When the problem is in the worker, she will either be onboard with the purpose, picture, plan, and participation, or working against it. The first group basically agrees with the stated purpose and plan, however, they are either slacking off and working below expectations, or working too hard, and perhaps controlling others too much. Very often, if someone is working below expectations, it may mean there is some problem in her participation. She may not feel meaningful to the purpose; she may need feedback, affirmation, or attention. These are the simplest cases to solve for they involve the rather pleasant task of affirming worth and encouraging people in their strengths. The controlling types need to be made aware of the limits of their authority.

The second group simply wants another purpose entirely and works actively or secretly against the leader. They will attempt to resist the changes planned. They may even attempt to replace the leader. They may not be aware of the commitment level of the leader and try to take advantage of what may seem like weak interest. They may strike at the very beginning when the plan is new, or wait for a moment of weakness later. In these cases it is most important to act quickly, especially if the person had some authority in the old system. Lines of authority cannot be shaky or uncertain in the new plan.

Some problems are caused by the leaders themselves. They are *iatrogenic*; that is, it is the leader's behavior that is the ultimate source of the crisis. *Iatrogenic*, a Greek-constructed word borrowed from medicine, refers to certain medical problems as having been "thrown" by the doctor at the patient. For example, a doctor in the operating room with the flu could himself be the cause of infection in the patient. The doctor is the actual source of the problem. It goes against all our ideas of proper medicine and is one of the last things anyone ever thinks about when contemplating a medical situation. It is last thought of in leadership as well, but worth considering. Iatrogenic problems happen, and wise leaders always consider the possibility of their own contribution to the event.

A wise leader asks, "What did I do or not do that might have contributed to this situation?" It is also wise to ask others if this is the case. After all, it is hard to be objective about your own behavior, especially in an emotional or sensitive case. It is also fair to ask the problem follower for input, just as an added source of feedback. If the leader senses some fault, and there is no one superior in charge, she might *imagine* how a person above her might respond. That would be a good time to honestly admit the fault and take steps to correct it. Only a leader with all of the qualities described in the section on character can do this. However, if done well, it can raise the credibility level of the leader's authority a great deal.

Finally, some problems will come from outside the immediate staff, or even outside the parish. They could be natural disasters, like an earthquake or fire, or a sudden economic change, or a public scandal. What these problems share is their public nature. Everyone knows about them and they are usually something of a newsworthy nature. That means people will talk, and leaders must also. If there is something big, obvious, and public going on in the neighborhood, and leaders do not speak about it, their hard-won credibility can disappear. Leaders must comment very soon about whatever is happening to remain credible as a person who is in charge, in the know, and able to cope. They must demonstrate their competence and capability to stay the course despite the crisis. They must demonstrate they still have the power to sail the ship through rough waters. Remember, information abhors a vacuum. If there is a crisis with no information coming from the top, people will supply their own with gossip, innuendo, and rumor. Who needs that!

Keeping a Calm Attitude

Clear thinking and a calm attitude are essential but difficult in a crisis. Short mnemonic words or phrases can help when everything crashes down at once. They settle us down enough to develop a clear plan. For example, the letters of the word *power* can help. *P* stands for *problem* and simply means the leader has an open attitude and will publicly acknowledge the problem right away. *O* stands for *opportunity* and means the leader has an attitude of hope and will show how this problem actually offers a real chance to make a change for the better. The problem has revealed an area that needs change and so we are grateful for the chance to improve. Of course, we wish the problem didn't happen at all, but now that it has we can use it to show our desire for improvement. *W* stands for a *winning attitude*. The leader next conveys an optimistic attitude that a solution is possible and within reach. This is crucial. People need to feel that someone is in charge and has a plan. This attitude demonstrates that the people, the parish, or the group are bigger than the problem. Again, it is a sense of hope in the future. *E* stands for *energize*. It goes along with the idea of winning and means the leader will work to energize the people toward the solution. Problems strike people in different ways and produce individual reactions. For some, problems are paralyzing. They collapse emotionally and give up hope. They become listless. The attitude of energy from the leader is a countersign to that and an important one. Words alone may not suffice to get the people on their feet, but personal example might. Finally, *R* stands for *resolve*. It means that the leader feels confident about the solution. He or she believes it will really work. It means the leader and people actually solve the problem. They fix it, improve it, and make it better.

Obviously, we cannot stop hurricanes or earthquakes, but we can institute this kind of effective recovery program for the problems that do occur in our churches and plan for such disasters in the future. Every crisis has some form of solution that makes the situation at least a little better. Working through the issue with the attitude of *power* ensures the leader retains the attitude of a leader and the people remain intact as followers. Good leaders acknowledge the problem, see an opportunity, project a winning confidence, energize the people, and resolve the situation.

Chapter Six

Caring for the People Who Follow

Ministry if it means anything at all means serving our people. It includes all the ideas presented so far that involve the leader-parishioner relationship, such as listening, respecting, and rewarding our people. Although it may seem strange to borrow a term that is so clearly from the secular business world, the ideas of *customer service* and *ministry* are very similar. In business the *motivation* to serve comes from a need to make money; however, the *motivation* in our ministry world is much deeper and more compelling. We *love* our people and want for them all the same goodness, grace, and love that Our Lord wanted for them also. Customer service is simply *loving our parishioners.*

Of course, understanding love is a big enough topic for any book, but we can certainly draw out a few ideas that are pertinent. Love is about giving. We can easily measure our relationships about love with that simple idea. At the end of the day we can ask ourselves a simple question, "How much was I concerned about 'getting' from others what was 'owed' to me, and how much was I involved in 'giving' to them? Did I pay attention to them, listen to their concerns, offer advice, spend time, provide help and support? Was I even interested in their lives?" Those answers can serve as a kind of measure of maturity and love.

This other-directed view of the world means we are able to see the world through the eyes of those we love. Our empathy is such that we can almost walk in their shoes and feel their experience. That makes serving so much easier. We have a deeper sense of what people need. It doesn't mean we can read minds, nor should we. It is always the responsibility of each of us to make our own needs known by ourselves. However, the intuition that comes from empathy and concern is helpful.

Love is life-giving. This famous phrase from the Marriage Encounter movement simply means we offer those things to our loved ones that increase their experience of authentic joy in life. We try to offer all that fulfills their true human nature. While drugs or crime may provide short-term benefits, they are beneath our dignity as persons, and so they are not loving gifts.

Love also respects the freedom of another. Recognizing the personal responsibility of each person before God to take charge of his or her life, we offer our help and support, never taking away that God-given autonomy. In this journey of life, we are fellow pilgrims walking together, not in place of each other. Our "giving" is never intrusive or invasive.

Love also means "receiving" in a balanced and mature way. Good leaders receive graciously and without embarrassment what others offer them as well. This mutual exchange involves intimacy. The deeper and more personal the sharing, the deeper the love grows.

Our parishioners are worthy of love. We express our love for them in some of the same ways that couples express their love for each other. We pay attention to them, anticipate their needs, take the time to listen, and offer what they need to enable their lives to be even more enjoyable.

Love cannot be secret, hidden, or invisible. We cannot read minds, nor should we try. Love must be expressed in ways the other person can understand. So also customer service is our way of publicly showing our love for our people. The way we act, respond, dress, speak, behave, work, and relate will express our love or lack of it to our people. All of the above actions are related to customer service, and they all are about real and practical love in ministry.

To check the level of love in the ordinary activities of service in the parish, we can look at a few general categories: people, pace, politeness, professionalism, and problems.

People

We can never take for granted that we "just know" our parishioners, or that leaders know their parish leaders. Nothing can take the place of actually finding things out directly. Certainly, the anecdotal information we receive from social occasions and the contact we make after the Masses on Sunday is helpful, but under those social situations sometimes etiquette prevents more realistic communication.

As we have seen already, taking the time to craft a careful survey of parishioner or ministerial concerns can be more accurate. After all, sometimes people are more honest when they are responding to a questionnaire than when they are looking at us directly. People are also impressed that we care enough to ask. It is vital afterward, of course, to share the results with them. Nothing kills cooperation the next time like forgetting to give feedback on the results the first time.

We should never presume we automatically know what is best for people. The more opportunities we provide for parishioner input that is respected, remembered, and responded to, the more united a parish becomes.

- Do we really know who our people are?

- Do we know something of the life they lead?

- Do we know their socioeconomic factors?

- Do we know what they want?

- Do we know what they need?

Pace

Waiting in line or in the front office lobby infuriates people at an alarming rate, especially when it is unexplained. Anger about waiting grows exponentially with each minute of our unexplained absence. A few minutes of mysterious delay signals disregard for people, and they feel it. Worse still, they remember. How many times does the office phone or doorbell ring before it is answered? How long does it take us to leave our office to meet with an appointment? Is the person informed of any delay, and how long approximately the delay will be? These are the concerns of pace and timeliness of our ministry.

People can tell very quickly if we want to be with them or not. A rushed attitude communicates disrespect and indifference and is condescending. It says our problem is not important. It is extraordinarily rude. What are we trying to communicate with a hurried demeanor? It can only come across as "Stay away! Don't talk to me!" It can also be a selfish desire to look busy when we are actually not in order to appear impressive and important. It counters any of the service we actually do perform no matter how good that service might be. People remember being rushed. Our service is about loving others, not ourselves.

- Is our service prompt and timely?

- Once delivered, does service seem too rushed and hurried?

Politeness

Because we live in rectories or work in Church offices all day we can become habituated to the surroundings. We easily forget many people might be arriving for an appointment for the first time. In fact, they might be coming to a Church office for the first time ever. Perhaps they are filled with all kinds of associations about that, or at least wonder if their concern will be addressed. The very building can communicate powerful ideas. What does the front of the office convey? Is there a welcoming sense to the entryway? Are there places to sit? Is it comfortable? What pictures are on the wall, and what do they communicate? What sounds are happening? For example, is there a radio blaring? classical music? traffic noise? Can we imagine what it must be like to come to our office? Of course, the most obvious part of hospitality is the appearance, demeanor, and behavior of the receptionists at the door, and their style of answering the phone. There can never be an excuse for rudeness anywhere.

- What does our parish entrance look like from a distance? from upclose?
- Is it clear where the offices are?
- How is the hospitality?
- Is there a welcoming attitude upon entering?
- What is it like to be asking for something here?
- How do we appear in dress, manner, and expression?
- Are there any countersymbols or actions around?

Professionalism

If parishioners see some service promoted either in the bulletin, or in the announcements, then we had better show up with the goods. Whether it is keeping our promised office hours, or starting and ending meetings on time, or executing stated projects, we must follow through on our word. Promises of service are like any promise, but especially here our word is being given to the people we love. We should honor it. Being professional is simply keeping our word. If we present ourselves at a certain level, let us keep it. Professionalism also means having clear boundaries between personal and public concerns. It means providing promised services despite our personal feelings about situations or people. It means being appropriately balanced in mixing our personal sense into parish or public concerns. After all, we came to serve, not to be served.

Finally, professionalism means completing the job. We can ask the person if they are satisfied and if there is anything else they need. If there is dissatisfaction we have the finest opportunity to love them.

- Are we doing what we say we are doing?
- Do we match all the services promised in the bulletin?
- Is the service complete?
- Does our service meet an "average" standard?
- Does our service meet our higher standard?
- Does our service have higher standards than the average?
- Is the person satisfied?

Problems

As we have seen, taking surveys for complaints is extremely helpful. After all, they tell us precisely where we can make improvements, and because so much joint planning went into setting the vision, it makes it easier *not* to take complaints personally. In fact, with so many people onboard, chances are the complaint will be from someone who has our best interests at heart, someone who is also committed to the same vision. The first step in handling complaints is to acknowledge them. That doesn't necessarily mean admitting blame. It simply means we heard the person and understand what the problem is. Second, offer a sad/glad–type comment: "We are sad this event happened, but we are glad you brought it to our attention." Next, ask what will make them happy. Let them set the parameters of service first. Finally, if possible and if reasonable, attempt some resolution. These ideas are simply common sense and flow from the basis of our unique style of Christian "customer service," which is simply and genuinely loving our parishioners. We love them as Our Lord first loved us.

- Do we know their complaints?
- Do we acknowledge we understand them?
- Do we offer a sad/glad response?
- Do we attempt to resolve the issue?
- Do we give an extra gift for free?

Chapter Seven

Conclusion

Although the Israelites suffered a great deal in Egypt, nothing much happened for a long time. Complaining and crying didn't change anything for them, and rebellion didn't work either. Nothing saps energy like the hopeless feeling of being stuck. The Israelites knew their life was terrible and anticipated no future. They longed for something different, but they didn't know how to get it. Only when Moses organized their thoughts, feelings, and actions behind a purpose, picture, and plan, with a part for everyone to play, did change occur.

The Exodus remains one of the most dramatic tales in human history, precisely because it touches on events we see every day. Organizations still become stuck in patterns that stifle growth and effective work. Like the Israelites we also know it's terrible, but we're not exactly sure what to do. Nothing saps energy like the feeling of being helpless and hopeless. Yet what worked for Moses was no accident. God knew what He was doing when He guided Moses through the steps of the Exodus. Each step worked because God works directly with human nature. After all, He designed us in just such a way that the actions Moses took would be effective with the people.

These ideas are not imposed on us arbitrarily. They are not some bureaucratic directive or organizational psychology trick that autocratically commands our behavior. We want these dynamics of God-inspired leadership in our life. These desires are built into our nature. The Exodus event worked precisely because God tapped into the very things people wanted deeply for themselves. After all, God knew they were there.

When a Moses in our own life looks into our eyes and announces, "We can do great things in this place. See how wonderful it will be! I know a way to get there, and I want you to join in me in making it happen. I have an important part for you to do. Let's make a real difference and move our people forward!" Deep down, we want to join with others in a great undertaking. We want to be part of a great and worthy project that transcends us. We are the most satisfied when we complete a project that is especially difficult and hard. Most especially, we also want to do well. We want to excel and to succeed. We will gladly join any effort that appeals to each of these factors. Moses used them all. We know the journey is long and seems more like a trek across a desert, but the result is worth it.

As Christians we take each step guided by *prayer*. That is the ultimate and final key motivation word and it underlies everything. Although we already appropriately discuss prayer frequently in various parish gatherings, these more secular ideas on motivation are rarely heard. This book simply wants to include them in an already well-developed spiritual formation program. The four key words of purpose, picture, plan, and participation complete the process.

Our faith history reveals stories of movement for various *communities of persons*, such as Adam and Eve in the Garden of Eden, the Israelites in Egypt, the development of the Twelve Apostles, or the growth of the Church itself. The latest story is the story being written in your parish. God is calling you to come forth from the community and to lead people in fulfilling His plan. In a way, God is saying that his plan *will not happen automatically*. You must play your part. Let us all simply learn from the lessons he implanted in our hearts and in our nature, the lessons that he has shown us so often in our history.

If our present situation represents any problem, if we think things could be better, if we are unsure of what to do all day, let us look to our own successful salvation history. If we are confused by ambiguous roles, or the bewildering variety of leadership styles, if we feel we are not moving forward and are stuck in a hopeless bureaucratic mess, let us call forth the spirit of Moses again, and inspired by his example, let us move as a people to the "land flowing with milk and honey."

Resources for Preaching and Teaching

PARABLES OF CONVERSION
Homilies and Stories Based on the Lectionary
Lou Ruoff

Paper, 128 pages, 5.5" x 8.5", ISBN: 0-89390-403-1

To make a point about conversion, look into *Parables of Conversion*. Some are narratives, others more poetic. Some are dialogue, others are reflections that occur only within one's heart of hearts. Some are fantasy, others help you experience what it is like to live in the gutter with the muck of humanity. But each tale relates a set of experiences that lead, through grace, to a moment of conversion. And each parable poses a spiritual question while remaining open-ended — to encourage discussion and reflection.

THE DREAM CATCHER
20 Lectionary-Based Stories for Teaching and Preaching
James L. Henderschedt

Paper, 128 pages, 5.5" x 8.5", ISBN:0-89390-339-6

Dreams drive us to be better and better. This book will energize those dreams that are alive — and call back those lost and forgotten dreams. Reflection questions are included with each story.

WINDOWS INTO THE LECTIONARY
Seasonal Anecdotes for Preaching and Teaching
Donald L. Deffner

Paper, 160 pages, 5.5" x 8.5", ISBN: 0-89390-393-0

Too often, anecdotes fall flat because they a) don't fit the reading, b) don't connect to real life, c) make simplistic analogies, or d) don't have a punchline. No such problem with this collection. Homiletics professor Donald Deffner has made a significant effort to locate short sermon illustrations that work on all levels. This collection packs a punch. The illustrations carry a universal spiritual truth that can be applied to the hearer's personal world. Many stories have a telling climax. All of them are connected to the church year — and there is an index that enables you to search for stories by season, theme, or scripture verse.

See the last page for ordering information

More Preaching Resources

EXTRAORDINARY PREACHING
20 Homilies by Roman Catholic Women

Edited by Rosalyn Karaban, PhD and Deni Mack, DMin

Paper, 96 pages, 5.5" x 8.5", ISBN: 0-89390-390-6

You dont have to be ordained to be invited to preach. You just have to be good. The women who gave the sermons in *Extraordinary Preaching* are good and in demand. At retreat houses. At priestless parishes. At interdenominational chapels. At memorial services and weddings. People want to know where they are preaching next. Their homilies are concrete and colorful. They link the Scripture stories with the blood, bones, and dirty dishes of ordinary life. And they have various personal styles from academic, to pastoral, to storytelling. These homilies will inspire you and show you what can be done from any pulpit.

STORY POWER!
Compelling Illustrations for Preaching and Teaching

James A. Feehan

Paper, 120 pages, 5.5" x 8.5", ISBN: 0-89390-304-3

To really get your point across you've got to tell stories. Good ones. Short ones. Powerful ones. Stories that intrigue. Stories that fascinate. Stories that capture the imagination. And then your stories have to hook your listeners to the gospel message. These anecdotes and quick story illustrations meet that challenge.

HOMILY RESOURCES
From Celebrating The Lectionary (CTL)

Edited by Liz Montes

Looseleaf, 312 pages, 8.5" x 11" Published annually in August

Helpful reflections on the Sunday readings that help you think without telling you what to think. Use independently or coordinate with the CTL curriculum. Covers every Sunday of the year from the first Sunday in September through the last Sunday in August.

See the last page for ordering information

Stories for Faith Sharing

LORD YOU MUST BE JOKING
Bible Stories That Tell Your Story
Eugene Webb

Paper, 176 pages, 5.5" x 8.5", ISBN: 0-89390-309-4
Leaders Guide: Paper, 80 pages, 5" x 8", ISBN: 0-89390-310-8

Here are stories set into a biblical context with a twist that makes you think. Reflection questions help the process. Use the leaders guide for retreats or other group situations.

STORIES TO INVITE FAITH-SHARING
Experiencing the Lord Through the Seasons
Mary McEntee McGill

Paper, 128 pages, 5.5" x 8.5", ISBN: 0-89390-230-6

Sharing our stories makes our faith journey easier. These twenty stories are based on real life experiences which help us recognize God's presence in everyday life. Reflections and questions for group sharing can lead to personal awareness and prayer. Great for faith-sharing groups, workshops, and retreats.

DEEPDOWN SPIRITUALITY
Seasonal Stories That Invite Faith-Sharing
Joseph J. Juknialis

Paper, 144 pages, 5.5" x 8.5", ISBN: 0-89390-392-2

Joseph J. Juknialis, a popular and imaginative storyteller, has turned his hand to real-life personal stories that work especially well for faith-sharing groups. This is a collection of poetic/prose reflections on the Sunday Scriptures throughout the three cycles of the lectionary. Topical and seasonal indices help you select the right story for the right time.

See the last page for ordering information

Hone Your Storytelling Skills

STORYTELLING STEP BY STEP

Marsh Cassady, PhD

Paper, 156 pages, 5.5" x 8.5", ISBN: 0-89390-183-0

Marsh Cassady, a director, actor, and storyteller, shows you all the steps to successful storytelling: selecting the right story for your audience, adapting your story for different occasions, analyzing it so that you can present it well, preparing your audience, and presenting the story. Includes many examples of stories.

CREATIVE STORYTELLING

Marsh Cassady, PhD

Three Audio Cassettes

These audio cassettes are adapted from the authors books *Storytelling Step-By-Step* and *Creating Stories for Storytelling*. Learn all the steps to successful storytelling: selecting the right story for your audience, adapting your story for different occasions and audiences, analyzing it, preparing your audience, and presenting the story. Youll also find ideas for creating your own original stories, plotting a story, creating tension, and writing dialogue that will keep your listeners on the edge of their chairs. The authors theatrical experience helps the example stories take on a life of their own.

CREATING STORIES FOR STORYTELLING

Marsh Cassady, PhD

Paper, 144 pages, 5.5" x 8.5", ISBN: 0-89390-205-5

This book picks up where the author's popular *Storytelling Step by Step* left off. Includes ideas for creating your own original stories, adapting stories to different audiences, plotting a story, creating tension, and writing dialogue that will keep your listeners on the edge of their chairs.

See the last page for ordering information

Resources for Parish Administration

SACRAMENTAL REGISTER WITH CERTIFICATE MAKER
Diskettes, for Windows 3.1 or higher, $99
Demo diskette available or download the demo for free at:
http://www.rpinet.com/software.html

Need a quick way to look up information on the sacrament reception records in your parish? Don't want to spend an arm and a leg? Try *Sacramental Register*. This Windows program makes data entry simple and information retrieval a snap. Log names, addresses, key dates, and register locations. Search names and dates easily. As a bonus, print out beautiful certificates for the enquirer. Data can be exported for use in other programs. The sacraments and ceremonies tracked are: rite of acceptance into the catechumenate, Baptism, Confirmation, first Communion, profession of faith, and Marriage.

ECO-CHURCH
An Action Manual
Albert J. Fritsch, SJ, with Angelaladavaia-Cox

Paper, 150 pages, 8.5" x 11",ISBN: 0-89390-206-3

Your parish can help save the earth! You can clean up your facilities, buy green supplies, make your worship more sensitive to the needs of the earth, and help the members of your parish assess their lifestyles. Great for Art and Environment committees.

See the last page for ordering information

Liturgy Planning Software

LITURGY PLUS
CD-ROM, for Windows 3.1 or higher — Site License
Demo diskette available or download the demo for free from:
http://www.rpinet.com/software.html

This easy-to-use program gives you a perfect script for every Sunday and major feast by default. With a click of the mouse you can pick different options. Then click your mouse again for a printout. In a few seconds, you've got a perfect script that you can deliver to your presider or planning committee. Plus, you can review, print out, or copy to your word processor dozens of commentary files on the lectionary, the sacramentary, the environment, music, and more. Templates help you plan each service and write general intercessions appropriate to your own community. Now includes RCIA.

Order from your local bookseller, or contact:

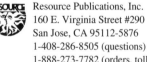
Resource Publications, Inc.
160 E. Virginia Street #290
San Jose, CA 95112-5876
1-408-286-8505 (questions)
1-888-273-7782 (orders, toll-free)
1-408-287-8748 (fax)
info@rpinet.com
www.rpinet.com

NG